MARY,

MYSTERY OF MERCY

Mary,

Mystery of Mercy

by

Marie-Dominique Philippe, O.P.

John Paul II Institute of Divine Mercy
An imprint of Marian Press
Marians of the Immaculate Conception
Stockbridge, Massachusetts 01262

Nihil Obstat:
Rev. Richard J. Drabik, M.I.C.
Provincial Censor
May 7, 2002

Imprimi Potest (English Translation):
Very Rev. Walter M. Dziordz, M.I.C.
Provincial Superior
May 9, 2002

Library of Congress Catalog Number: 2002104167

ISBN: 0-944203-75-2

Editor: Robert Stackpole, STD
Typesetting: Patricia Menatti
Cover Design: William Sosa

Special thanks: to Mr. Shaun Hillary, for his generous support
and prayers

Front Cover: The Image of Our Lady, the Mother of Mercy, without its silver garments and crowns, venerated in the Chapel above the Dawn Gate in the city of Vilnius, Lithuania, where the first Image of Jesus, The Divine Mercy, painted according to St. Maria Faustina's description, was first seen by the public in 1935.

Published by:
John Paul II Institute of Divine Mercy
An imprint of Marian Press
Marians of the Immaculate Conception
Stockbridge, Massachusetts 01262

Table of Contents

3. Annunciation

Preface

Marie-Dominique Philippe, O.P.

It has now been over 40 years since I began to consider the mystery of Mary in the light of the Father's mercy, thinking that the best way to enter her mystery was perhaps to see that she was totally fashioned and educated, and "determined," by the Father's mercy. In this sense I sought to specify the particular characteristics of this mercy, in all of the mysteries of her life. At that time, I had wanted to give a series of lectures on the Father's mercy vis-a-vis Mary — from the first, initial mercy found in the mystery of the Immaculate Conception to the ultimate mercy found in the mystery of the Assumption. I had wanted to consider, in each of the periods of Mary's life (the joyous mysteries and the sorrowful mysteries), this mercy of the Father with respect to her: His gaze as Father upon His little child, which is "pure gaze", so to speak. With respect to us, mercy consists in purifying "poor sinners", for, in us, mercy has been damaged, stained; mercy in us has not the limpidity, the purity that it has in Mary. What is wonderful regarding Mary is that we find ourselves before mercy received (be it consciously or unconsciously — for the mercy of the Immaculate Conception was received unconsciously) in all purity, such mercy in no way being damaged by anything. In Mary, nothing countered the Father's mercy. His mercy could be exercised with unique purity.

I thus began with the mysteries of the Immaculate Conception, the Presentation, and the Annunciation. The advantage of considering all three of these mysteries is that we can see more clearly how Mary was educated by the Father in and through mercy. If one day I have the time, I hope to consider the Father's mercy in the other mysteries of Mary's life.

It is very important for us to understand that the Father gazes upon us always through His mercy, and in His mercy. His gaze is not primarily one of justice, seeing whether or not we are in conformity with law. Mercy surpasses the law. The surpassing is an absolute. Mercy goes further than the law. If Jesus says that he comes to accomplish, to fulfill the law, it is because Jesus is perfectly united to the Father. He is one with the Father. Consequently, he enters this fatherly mercy perfectly. Jesus continues this fatherly mercy and adapts it for and to us. The mercy of Jesus brings the law to completion, without suppressing it. If the mercy of Jesus were to suppress the law, it would not be mercy. The law is not suppressed, but rather reaches its perfection. It is developed in an infinitely greater sense, where love envelops and takes hold of everything. This is true for all the saints, but for Mary, it is eminently and perfectly true.

Mary never diminished the Father's action in her. She never betrayed the Father's merciful action in her. Mary understood and loved perfectly this merciful action. In this consists her holiness. Mary's holiness consists in having received all of the mercies of the Father in an absolutely perfect fashion, with total limpidity, without diminshing them. This is wonderful. Nowadays, in the great struggles that we endure, the Devil is particularly furious, for his days are numbered; and he knows that the Second Coming is closer than it was 2000 years ago. He knows that, at the Second Coming, he will be rendered impotent viv-a-vis humanity. He will be obliged to return to the "place" prepared for him.

The Father gives His mercy to Mary, in increasingly superabundant fashion. He enlarges Mary's heart, enabling her to go always further in mercy. The Devil does just the opposite. He tries to lead us to that which hinders the Father's mercy in us, damaging, limiting, and reducing it to his own dimensions, those of a being who has rebelled against God's mercy. The mercy of God with respct to Mary is so great and so strong that it is unbearable for the Devil. To understand this rage of the Devil, and his "furious" action upon us, it suffices to consider the Father's mercy for Mary, His little child.

That is why it seemed beneficial to present these three "mysteries of mercy", originally published in three separate books in 1958, edited and newly published in a single book (in French) in 2000, and now published in English. We see with great force how the Father educates Mary through His mercy. Mary has been given to us as mother, so that we might live the same mystery as her. The following pages propose just that: to live the same mystery as Mary. May these, her mysteries, help us to live the Father's mercy, and make of our lives an unceasing canticle of thanksgiving: "I will sing the mercies of Lord forever." (Psalm 88)

Introduction

Born in 1912 in Cysoing, in northern France, Marie-Dominique Philippe came from a large family, whose prayerfulness played an important role for him, and his siblings. Indeed, seven of the twelve children entered the religious life. His passion as a youngster was mathematics. Nevertheless, he entered the Dominican Order in 1930, in the footsteps of his older brother, Père Thomas (co-founder of the L'Arche community with Jean Vanier) ... largely influenced by his Dominican uncle, Père Pierre-Thomas Dehau (then spiritual director for Raissa Maritain). He made his religious profession in 1931, and was ordained to the ministerial priesthood in July of 1936.

Fr. Philippe was sent as a professor to the (Pontifical, Dominican) University of Fribourg (Switzerland) in 1945, where he taught full time until 1982. Although preoccupied with what he believed God was asking of him through his religious community, his teaching/preaching "career" afforded him a variety of enriching encounters with the likes of persons such as theologians Marie-Dominique Chenu, O.P. and Henri De Lubac, S.J., artists George Rouault and Paul Claudel, thinkers Etienne Gilson and Jean Guitton, and scientists, politicians, religious leaders and psychoanalysts and ... .

Impassioned by the search for truth at all levels, Fr. Philippe has labored incessantly for the acquisition of wisdom. Recognizing the great autonomy of the human intellect (which he sees as an expression of the respect the Creator has for his creature), he has developed, with as much precision as possible, the three wisdoms of which man is capable: philosophical, theological, and spiritual (or mystical), a distinction found in Thomas Aquinas, and more recently reiterated in *Fides et Ratio*, published by John Paul II in 1998. Fr. Philippe is indeed an original thinker. His tremendous love for Thomas Aquinas does not, as one discovers upon closer reading, inscribe him in the "good old Scholastic Tradition." As his confrère, Aidan Nichols, O.P., from Great Britain suggests, Fr. Philippe is unclassifiable. "Fr. Philippe," he says "extends the tradition of the 'vision' of Thomas Aquinas by creatively transforming it. I think he will one day come to be regarded as a major inspiration in late twentieth, early twenty-first century Francophone Catholicism." Fr. Philippe is a man interested in anyone who seeks truth, no matter how different his or her background may be. "All seekers of truth are friends," as he likes to say.

His professorial role was that of a philosopher, having held a chair in Metaphysics. That would seem to make him an unlikely candidate for the foundation of a new religious order, the Congregation of Saint John (founded in 1975). The foundation of the Brothers of Saint John (and later, two branches of nuns — contemplative in 1982, and apostolic in 1984) was not something Fr. Philippe had intended, and for which, consequently, he was not preparing. As he says, "I had *never* thought of it, ever. It's very simple, in fact: the Congregation of Saint John was asked of me. It was not something I had willed. It was a small group of my students who approached me."[1] Fr. Philippe's initial reaction was understandably one of hesitancy. It was clear to him that nothing new was necessary. Or so he thought.

The new foundation, in retrospect, was indeed an unusual thing: a new community, founded by a Dominican, in a Dominican setting, that was not Dominican. There is, of course, an inevitable kinship. When asked of the connection, Fr. Philippe responds, "I absolutely do not wish the Congregation of Saint John to be a rival of the Order of Saint Dominic. They are different. Seen from without, in a sociological fashion, the difference may seem subtle, and therefore difficult to detect. Indeed, *agens agit simile sibi*: can a Dominican found anything that is not a certain prolongation, or extension, of the Dominican Order? And yet, if one is truly a founder, that is, if it is God who is asking, and it is not a personal decision (as would be the case with someone who always dreamed of founding an order that would correspond to what he dreams), then one is, above all, an

---

1. *Les Trois Sagesses*, Fayard, Paris, 1994

instrument of the Holy Spirit; and the Holy Spirit can have spring, from a Dominican, a Brother of Saint John!" He continues, "The Congregation of Saint John is not a reform of the Order of Saint Dominic. I never thought along those lines. I never positioned myself as a reformer. But, in my life, I have been careful to try to highlight the sources, the deep intention of Saint Dominic: his concern to 'speak only with God and of God' and his great thirst for truth. His thirst for truth, for light, and a very penetrating gaze upon the mystery of Jesus crucified, always seemed to me to be the deep secret of Saint John. And the way in which Saint Thomas Aquinas speaks of the holiness of Saint John always seemed to me to be what characterizes his own holiness, that of a son of Saint Dominic."[2]

As a son of Saint Dominic himself, Fr. Philippe is an intimate son of Mary, the love for whom he shares with his sons, the Brothers of Saint John, and anyone else willing to listen. His philosophical inquiry and research has, interestingly enough, served this communication. From the age of six, Fr. Philippe read for his uncle, Fr. Dehau, who was going blind. As a novice, on a visit to his uncle, a visit during which he continued a reading of Aristotle, he was given wise counsel: "You must enter deeply into metaphysics, for metaphysics enables us to speak of Mary. You must study metaphysics to be able to speak of Mary, and to communicate her to others."

Indeed, who is Mary? She is a mystery, a mystery of mercy, for she has been enveloped by God … and given to us. "Mary is the masterpiece of God at the Cross. She is the masterpiece of God, of the Father, and the Holy Spirit, *for us*. The one who is given to us is the *Woman*, who is one with Jesus crucified. And she who is entirely turned towards Jesus is entirely turned towards us, and is given to each one of us in a unique way. We must receive her. We must ask the Holy Spirit to grant us a divine experience of the heart of Mary, who is our desert."[3]

2. *Les Trois Sagesses*, Fayard, Paris, 1994
3. *J'ai Soif*, Editions Saint Paul, Versailles, 1996

Mary, Mystery of Mercy

1

Immaculate Conception

Immaculate Conception

Mary is given to us as the masterpiece of God's mercy, as she whose primary role it is to have us enter through the narrow and royal door of the Father's mercy.

Because Mary is truly the masterpiece of mercy, she is, so to speak, the Father's mercy personified. In God, mercy is an attribute. In Mary, God's mercy "is" Mary. What I mean is that everything in her is mercy. There is nothing but mercy in her; that is why she is truly the Father's mercy personified. In God, mercy is an attribute because the mystery of God *per se* is beyond mercy. The mystery of the Father and of the Son and of the Holy Spirit, the mystery of the Trinity, is a mystery of Gift, a Gift of love, a pure Gift in which there is only love. The Father wishes for this love to be communicated to us and, for this, there needs be the great "bridge" of mercy, as Catherine of Siena[1] calls it.

One might object that mercy personified is Jesus, to which I respond, "Yes and no." We must understand that because Christ Himself is God, His mystery is beyond mercy. The Father has placed His "good pleasure" in Jesus. However, as Thomas Aquinas tells us, in Jesus, human nature, strictly speaking, is assumed. It is not a creature.[2] With this we understand how Jesus is not an object of the Father's mercy, for the Father's mercy is only exercised toward creatures. Jesus is the source of mercy for us, but, in His intimate relationship with the Father, He is beyond mercy, for He is the only Son of the Father. *Vis-à-vis* the Son, the Father does not have an attitude of mercy, but an attitude of love. That is why, on the Cross, Jesus can accomplish an act of justice in the highest sense, that is, plenary satisfaction for our faults. He is the Beloved Son. It is a relationship of "filiation" which unites Him to the Father. This unique rela-

---

1. Italian mystic, Dominican tertiary, 1347-1380.
2. St. Thomas Aquinas, *Summa Theologica (ST)* III. q. 16, a. 8 & 10, q. 20, a 1, ad. 1.

tionship of filiation is founded upon the eternal procession, upon the eternal generation in the Trinity.

Mary, however, is a creature, and only a creature. Mercy, therefore, envelops her from the beginning, totally and completely. Throughout her life she unceasingly receives the fullness of God's mercy. This mercy is destined to introduce her into love, but a love with a particular nuance: when the love of God is communicated to a creature, it necessarily takes the form of mercy.

This is important to understand, for Mary is given to us as a mother, as a model. She is given to us that we might live the same mystery as she lives. If we understand how Mary is the Father's mercy personified for us, how she is the masterpiece of this mercy, we will have, in a certain sense, the key to penetrating and living all the mercies of the Father. In fact, we cannot live by the Father's mercy in a complete fashion if we do not live in Mary, if we do not have this full intimacy with her.

The Father's mercy is, as it were, totally communicated to Mary. It is obvious that the cause always contains more than its effect. Mary is never identified with God. However, this being so, mercy was full and complete in her, mercy was communicated to her without limit. We can thus say that all that God possesses in His own being in a substantial way, Mary possesses by grace in a participated way. In other words, she possesses it vitally. All that the Father is, Mary lives. The grace accorded to Mary draws her close to the mystery of the Trinity[3] in a unique way.

In order to better understand the value of the gift that Jesus gives at the Cross, it can be useful for us to consider all of the mysteries of Mary in the light of the Father's mercy. We must not look at the mysteries of Mary in themselves, but as effects of the Father's mercy. Each of the mysteries of Mary is for us a doorway, as it were, a great light in the midst of darkness, a great flash of lightning, a great tearing of the veil, which enable us to penetrate and live the Father's mercy, to surrender completely and rest in the Father's mercy.

3. *ST* III q. 27, a. 5, ad. 1

Part One

Father of Mercy

Mercy: Path to God

It is good to recall briefly what mercy is, that is, to place ourselves in the light of mercy.

Mercy is not the "mystery" of God considered in itself. Mercy is not God considered in His personal mystery. Mercy is the "attribute" of God *par excellence*. It is the attribute whereby we can live the mystery of God in the deepest way. We indeed say "live" and not "know", for, from a speculative viewpoint, the first of the attributes of God is simplicity. Simplicity is more impressive for the intellect. We could say that simplicity is the attribute of God *par excellence* for our intellect as philosophers or as theologians. To little children, however, Jesus says, "There are secrets given neither to the wise nor the learned."[4] To the wise is given this wonderful *via*, this wonderful path: penetrating the mystery of God through His simplicity. This royal path immediately places our intellects as theologians into a state of contemplation.

But when it comes to the mystery of God, love can go further than the intellect. Charity, although lived in faith, surpasses faith. That is why our hearts as Christians penetrate the mystery of God more deeply than our intellects as theologians, as subtle as the latter may be. A path of access, a special doorway to the mystery of God is given to little children, that of God's mercy. In the light of mercy we can contemplate the whole mystery of God, and penetrate it very intimately. For this to occur, however, we must live this mercy. We must let ourselves be enveloped by it completely, which demands an attitude of great humility. Contemplation of God in and through His mercy is indeed the contemplation of "little ones" who know not how to be anything by themselves and who receive everything gratuitously.

4. Mt 11:25-26; Lk 10:21

Mercy: Father's Love

If we examine just what mercy is, we see that it has as its principle, and demands, an excessive love. To be merciful is to love superabundantly, to love in an excessive fashion, as though possessing the very source of love. If we are not a source of love, we cannot be merciful. One who is not a source of love has a partial love, has a particular love, and, consequently, cannot communicate it to those who need it, cannot give it fully without calculation. Mercy demands that we give fully without calculation, for the moment we begin to calculate, it is no longer mercy. In order to be merciful, we must be in the realm of "first (primary) love." We must possess nobility and grandeur regarding love. This is precisely what we contemplate in the mystery of the Father.

I intentionally say the mystery *of the Father*. It is, of course, the mystery of God which is the source of love, but note that, in the mystery of God, there is yet a very hidden source, a source whence comes the mystery of the Trinity. The mystery of mercy indeed comes from the mystery of God, but our gaze as little children seeks to go further and investigate the abyss of *the Father's* mercy. It is the Father's mercy which "preoccupies" us, which concerns us. With respect to this mercy, a little child has, as it were, "divine vertigo". He ardently desires to plunge and to lose himself in the abyss, for it is precisely there and only there that we are face-to-face with the source. Mercy can only be perfectly itself when it flows from the source of love. Mercy is great love, full love, superabundant love. It is through experience of the Father's mercy that we understand the nobility and grandeur of the Father. It is through experience of the Father's mercy that we understand the unfathomable abyss of His love.

Mercy: Power at the Service of Love

If we consider how God reveals His mercy in Scripture, we see that He manifested Himself first as omnipotent Creator, then as loving Father. This is normal, for mercy presupposes omnipotence and goodness. In order to be merciful, we must not only be good, but omnipotent in goodness. That is why mercy is, as it were, a divine synthesis of these two first attributes (first, not according to the order of perfection, but according to the order of manifestation to us). Indeed, for our human intellect which knows God through the grandeur of His sensible effects, omnipotence is first. We first discover God as First Cause. The First Cause is necessarily omnipotent and infinite in efficacy. Every existent reality immediately depends upon this Cause. That is why our practical intellect always returns to the omnipotence of the Creator as its only support for its practical and religious demands. Hence, the revelation of His omnipotence is the first truth that God reveals in so far as we are rational creatures capable of reaching Him intellectually. Moreover, since we are created in the image of God, our first likeness with the Creator is participation in His power. God communicates to man *dominion* over the whole universe. Man was to be able to eat of the fruit of all the trees except the Tree of Life.[5]

It is not only the omnipotence of the Creator that is manifested in God's image, but also the love and goodness of the Father. Creating man in His image[6] means that God wishes to communicate to him His intimate life. Communication of life is the act proper to the Father. That is why the second quality that God imprints on His image is the capacity to love. God gave Eve to Adam so that Adam might be able to speak with and love a being like himself, drawn from himself and in the image of God.[7] Adam has the power to dominate the universe and the power to love his spouse. He is thereby the echo of the omnipotent Creator and infinitely good Father, for the quality proper to a father, as such, is goodness with respect to his children. The Father communicates His goodness; He communicates his love.

These indeed are the first two elements, the first two poles, so to speak, of the revelation of the mystery of God: the omnipotence of the Creator and the goodness of the Father. However, because of sin, the goodness of the Father is, as it were, rejected by man. Out of pride man no longer wishes to

5. Gn 1:28-32; 2:15-17
6. Gn 1:27; 2:7
7. Gn 2:20b-24

love and to experience the powerful attraction of the divine good and of His love. He distances himself from the goodness of the Father and from His love. The omnipotence of the Creator, who punishes in His anger, is all that remains visible to him; and so man no longer dares to gaze upon God. Man hides when God is present. He is ashamed of his nakedness.[8] He has uprooted love from his heart. Because of sin, the goodness of the Father and His love can no longer be reached by man, save through the Father's mercy. This act of the Father's mercy restores the prodigal son to the house of his Father. It is through mercy that we once again penetrate the inmost mystery of the Father's goodness.

Mercy is thus a "divine ladder." It implies omnipotence at the service of goodness and love. This is precisely what is proper to mercy. Possessing sovereignty, grandeur and nobility, the Creator stoops to us with the face of a father, with the acts of a father, with the solicitude of a father. The omnipotence of the Creator is at the service of His love in order to reach us in our inmost selves. As Creator, God is intimately present to all that is in us. In mercy, He places His omnipotence at the service of love in order to embrace us in our inmost being with His love. And when He places His omnipotence at the service of His love, God accomplishes the sovereign act of His mercy.

This is what God desires that we ourselves do when Jesus commands us to, "Be merciful as your Heavenly Father is merciful."[9] The Creator has placed in us a power. We are intelligent and we are strong. This intelligence and this strength vary from one individual to the next, but we all have the power to do something and each of us senses it in himself. We also have a heart capable of love.

The Sin of the World: Love at the Service of Power

The great tragedy for humanity these days, is that of having opted for power, of having placed love at the service of power. This is the Devil's strategy in his goal to overthrow the Father's

8. Gn 3:10-11; Cf Gn 2:25
9. Lk 6:36

work. Simply look around us and within us. We are children of this age, and we know that our deepest and most tragic struggles come from trying to dominate everything in one way or another. We have a horrible instinct for domination. It suffices to consider our need to criticize everything. Our first interior movement is often that of criticizing. Critical judgment and negative judgment stem from an instinct for domination. It is the most radical way to dominate. However, the moment we say "No" to something greater than us (to God's will for us, for example) we immediately close the door to love and opt for domination.

The strategy of the Devil consists in giving primacy to power over love, in having power pass before love, and even in placing love at the service of power, which, in fact, suppresses love. Love refuses to be at the service of power, for it is more than power. Love is more than domination. It is deeper and more divine. Love alone enables us to attain to our *end.* The minute we make of love a *means* we suppress it. In the supernatural realm, the primacy of love with respect to end is even clearer. Saint Augustine makes a distinction between *uti* (utilizing) and *frui* (enjoying). Love, he says, is *frui*.[10] If we place love on the side of *uti*, that is, on the side of service, of means, and not of end, we cause a terrible schism and disfigure God's work. The great tragedy of our time is that of having inverted the order of God's wisdom. We exalt power, efficiency, and production and we relativize love. Love is only considered to be an instinctive force; hence, just another power. God wants everything to be at the service of love so that everything might be renewed in mercy, so that everything might be brought to completion in mercy, so that mercy might have the last word.

For us, living in these times, we must become aware of this tragedy. God must be able to "set things right" in and through us. His mercy must be able to be fully realized in us. Power must always be at the service of love in us. The greater the natural power God gives to us as regards intellect, other faculties, *habitus*, virtue, various aptitudes, and qualities – not to mention

---

10. *De Doctrina Christiana* 1, 4, 4 P.L. 34, c. 20

the responsibilities that God gives to us – the more we must place all of these things at the service of love. If we proceed otherwise, we enter somewhat into the *mores*, the ways of the Devil, that is, the ways of the one who is anti-love. We then no longer have the ways of God, the ways of the Father. We adopt the ways of the one who opposes himself, the adversary.

It is important to understand these things when it comes to the Christian life, for the Christian life is the narrow door. Nowadays we must be all the more attentive because the slightest deviations in the contemplative life – be it the religious life or the Christian life "common" to all – come from this error. This is normal. After Adam's sin, slight deviations lead to enormous errors. A slight difference in orientation between two neighboring springs leads to two rivers which find themselves at a considerable distance from one another.

We need to understand that God's mercy must have the last word. Here we are at the root of the mystery of God for us. Here we stand before primal realities. The Father's mercy is the alpha and the omega. And if we reflect on it, we see that this mercy implies the Creator's omnipotence at the service of the Father's goodness.

The Mercy of Jesus: Manifestation of the Mercy of the Father

If we consider the Gospels we see clearly what we have hitherto expressed. The Son wants to reveal the Father to us. This is His unique and sole purpose[11]. How does He present Himself? When asked who He is, He takes up the prophetic words of Isaiah presenting the Messiah as the one who heals the sick, as the one who makes paralytics walk and the blind see, as the one, thanks to whom those who have no life begin to have it again.[12] These are the deeds, the acts, which define Jesus. They are acts of mercy. From time to time we observe an

---

11. Cf. Jn 1:18
12. See Mt 11:5; Lk 7:22; Is 26:19; 35:5-6; 61:1

act of justice, but the justice is at the service of mercy. If Jesus is severe with the Pharisees regarding their pride, it is in order to purify, to liberate us from the instinct for power which always risks making Pharisees of us too. All of Christ's acts are expressions of mercy. The encounter with the adulterous woman (in the Gospel of John) in which we see an act of forgiveness – the act of mercy *par excellence* – shows well who Christ is.[13] This extraordinary passage is one of the most moving in the Gospel. Saint Augustine commented upon it, underscoring how Jesus wants to teach us that justice is, as it were, "absorbed" by mercy.[14] Justice is still power. It is necessary, therefore, that it be at the service of mercy, at the service of love. How does mercy take possession of justice? How does it completely take hold of it? All those who clamor for justice are obliged to disappear. These protagonists of justice, of the law (understood in a strict and pharisaical manner, as opposed to mercy) are living on the level of time, not on the level of eternity. Mercy is eternal, as is divine justice in mercy. Christ, Mercy Itself, remains alone with misery. Such is the life of Christ. Such is the whole of the Gospel: mercy confronted with the misery of a "poor woman." Indeed, this "poor woman" symbolizes the whole of sinful humanity. This poor woman, alone, face-to-face with Christ, is entirely forgiven. Her misery is assumed by Mercy. In the end, there is nothing left but Mercy. When we reach heaven, there will be nothing but mercy in our soul. And here below, to the extent we live by the Father's grace, we must strive to see to it that there is nothing but mercy from the Father toward us.

13. See Jn 8:1-11
14. See Homilies on the Gospel according to St. John, XXXIII, 4-8.

Part Two

Mary: Masterpiece of Mercy

In the light of the masterpiece of the Father's mercy, Mary, we shall attempt to examine carefully the principle acts of His mercy, those which characterize it, in order to understand better where mercy is to be found, so that we, in our Christian life, might penetrate it more deeply.

The first act of the Father's mercy with respect to Mary is an act of absolute gratuitousness. Hence, we see in this act the Father's mercy in all its purity. This first act is the Father's prevenient mercy for Mary as a tiny child in the womb, regarding the first movement of her soul: the mystery of the Immaculate Conception.

We must try to understand the mystery of the Immaculate Conception not only in itself, but in its source which is the mystery of the Father's prevenient mercy. There can be no mercy more absolute or more complete. Thomas Aquinas speaks of prevenient mercy as a particular act of mercy. Prevenience is, in fact, what characterizes mercy[15] (from the Latin *prae venire*: to come before).

If we want to understand what prevenient mercy is and what it means for us, we must consider the mystery of the Immaculate Conception: the first fruit of prevenient mercy, its fruit *par excellence*. Thus, the Immaculate Conception must enable us to penetrate this special abode of the Father's mercy.

Because He is merciful, the Father takes the initiative – He always takes the initiative. He is always "before", "ahead of" us. Because of the Father's infinite solicitude, and because the light of His mercy is His eternal gaze, mercy prepares and envelops everything.

Creation: First Act of Mercy

Let us explore the first act of prevenient mercy towards Mary.

---

15. *ST* I-II, q. 111, a. 3; cf Ps 59:10: *Misericordia ejus praevenit me.*

We shall then try to see its consequences. If we look in Scripture, we see that God, as Creator, as Creator of Adam and Eve, certainly performs an act of mercy. Creation is an act of mercy, for God creates out of pure, generous and gratuitous love. Creation is not a necessity for God. God creates out of pure superabundance, not to fulfill Himself. We, however, sometimes need to create, to make something. We have certain interior "urges", or "creative impulses" which need to be stated and expressed. Verbal expression is to "make something". There is a certain creation in speaking. There is, as it were, a distant echo of God's creative word. God creates through His word. "God said, and so it was."[16] We have within us the power to speak, and when we speak, we have the impression that we are creating.

There is something true in this, something which is particularly pronounced in the case of poets. Often poets exaggerate in this sense, but their exaggerations help us to understand what underlies human words, that is, the "urge" to speak. If, when we have a marvelous idea, or have seen or understood something astonishing, we encounter a friend, we have an irresistible desire to tell him about it. In point of fact, the spoken word, verbal language, is a "reflection" of God's act of Creation. This is one of the reasons why we ought to have great respect for the spoken word. We do not have a right to lie or falsify human words, for they prolong God's creation.[17]

Speaking is a natural necessity for us. For this reason, it can sometimes be difficult, quite difficult to check this need, especially for persons with artistic or poetic temperaments. For such persons it can be very much a necessity to speak.

If God creates, it is not at all out of natural necessity. This we know by faith. God creates out of pure liberality and, therefore, out of pure mercy. The first act of God's mercy is that of Creation. "In the beginning, God created the heavens and the earth." On the sixth day God made man in his own likeness.[18] God created our soul by an act of pure mercy, for we have no right, strictly speak-

16. Gn 1:6
17. Cf. Ex 20:16
18. See Gn 1:26-27

ing, to life. We have received everything from this fundamental mercy, the mercy of the Creator. It is substantial mercy, for it communicates life, intellect, and autonomy in being. It creates, starting from nothingness, and for this reason it is the first "gushing forth" of the mercy of the Father.

If we look at how Adam and Eve were created, we can see that, in a single act of mercy, God created soul and body—as Scripture shows it.[19] Because He wills to bring forth His masterpiece, and because He wills to make a being in His own image and likeness, God, in a single act of mercy, creates soul and body, and even more profoundly, He confers grace. For Adam and Eve there was only one birth, a wholly divine birth. Here we find the marvelous prevenient mercy of the Father, the act most connatural to God, Creator and Father. God wills to make something great, something in His own image and likeness, and so brings to realization a unique masterpiece by an act of prevenient mercy, of substantial mercy. Indeed, we must frequently return to the passage of Scripture which shows this act of the Father, fashioning man out of pure, gratuitous love, out of pure mercy.

Original Sin: Attack on Mercy

Man's first response to the Father's act of prevenient mercy, as Scripture recounts it, is an act of pride. God conferred upon man an extraordinary gift, that is, the possibility of being free to love, of being autonomous in his life. Man can do with it whatever he wills. He can either place the power God has given him at the service of love, or he can place love at the service of his own freedom and power. Man's first sin, original sin, is disobedience through pride; it is the exaltation of his autonomy. Eve allowed herself to be seduced, allowed herself to be taken in, and Adam later allows himself to be persuaded.[20]

Sin is a direct attack against the prevenient mercy of the Father. To sin is not to understand this prevenient mercy. It is to reduce it to our level, to bring it down to manageable size. In a

19. Gn 2:7
20. Gn 3:1-6

way, it is to want to monopolize and exploit it according to our pride, and our desire for autonomy, our desire to be independent of God. Sin is a direct attack on mercy. This is normal, for God envelops man from the start with His mercy. For Adam and Eve everything was mercy. They were wrapped in the mercy of God. They belonged totally to God. God watched over them. They came forth from His hands. God prepared for their human bodies an environment connatural to them; and the souls in their bodies were akin to God, and were directed toward God.

Instead of responding to His mercy with love with an act of submission and abandonment, Adam and Eve disobeyed out of pride. It was Eve who first allowed herself to be seduced by pride, by a desire for power. She allowed herself to be seduced by the false prophecy of the Serpent, by his fallacious promises; and she responded. She fell into the trap he was setting for her, namely that of curiosity, the curiosity of speaking to a spirit more powerful than she, and who was questioning her. Such is the strategy of temptation, which is marvelously revealed to us in Scripture. We are always flattered when someone greater than us questions us and seems to want to learn or receive something from us. We are all flattered by this and we fall into the trap. In all curiosity there is a certain seduction regarding someone greater than us who seems to be begging a parcel of truth. Eve began to respond... and we know the consequences.[21]

The consequences were permitted by God. All of the descendants of Adam and Eve, instead of being born in a state of original justice, would thenceforth receive from their parents nothing more than a human nature in a state of weakness and corruption. Adam and Eve are the first, the heads of human nature, "in charge". That is why their offense is so grave. Our own sin, or that of our parents, does not entail consequences for descendants. This we know well. The New Testament says it specifically.[22] In the Old Testament certain statements could

21. Gn 3:14-19
22. See Jn 9:2-3

lead us to believe that the sin of parents affect their children.[23]
Jesus shows us that Christian grace is free in this regard.

Original Sin: Attack on Human Nature

Why does Adam's sin involve all of humanity? Because
Adam is responsible for humanity.[24] God willed that he should
be first, inasmuch as he is father. Because God created man in
His own image, it is necessary that something of the fatherhood
of God be in Adam. This something is precisely the fact that the
whole human race descends from Adam. All of humanity is
contained in him according to the plan of God's wisdom.
Because Adam is the principle, the head, because Adam is the
image of the Father's fatherhood and has authority over the
entire human race, which is contained in him, his sin necessarily affects each and every one of his descendants.

We have difficulty understanding this because we find ourselves with the consequences of the Fall. It is very difficult to
go back as far as Adam! It is necessary to understand this from
God's perspective. If we look at it from God's perspective,
everything is simple and comprehensible. God established
Adam and Eve as the leaders of humanity. All of humanity,
therefore, being contained in them, was to depend upon them.
It is normal then that, if Adam and Eve thwart the mercy of
God, their descendants consequently be deprived of it. If they
prevent mercy from being complete, if they limit it (by sin we
limit the mercy of God) by means of the freedom with which
God has endowed them, this mercy is limited for their descendants. Adam and Eve do not destroy humanity. They could have
committed suicide. (Had they done so humanity itself would
have committed suicide.) God permitted this sin which places
an obstacle to the communication of divine life.

From the standpoint of nature, Adam and Eve remain the
heads of the human race, but heads who have lost their first
nobility. They did not know how to abide in the nobility in
which God had created them. They opposed the authority of

---

23. See Ex 20:5; Dt 5:9; 2 Sam 12:14
24. Thomas Aquinas specifies that if Adam had not sinned and only Eve had sinned
their descendants would not have contracted original sin because Adam is the
head of humanity in the full sense of the term. (Cf *ST* I-II, q. 81, a. 5)

God and rebelled against it. Since all of human nature is "in" them, it is to be expected that this nature, coming from them, should itself be in a fallen state; hence, we are born in a state of original sin. The state of original sin is nothing other than the transmission of the nature which sinned in Adam. Adam was the image of the Father. God had entrusted to him responsibility for humanity. Adam was not able fully to respect this image, and as a result, his descendants are marked with a natural defect. We are not responsible as *persons*, but as *nature* descending from Adam – for we possess the same nature as he did. We are responsible for the sin *in Adam and Eve*. We are not personally responsible, but our human nature bears this mysterious blemish.

This truth is one of the most difficult to accept today because contemporary existentialist philosophy exalts freedom and personhood in such a way as to refuse consideration of human nature. In such a perspective, original sin has no more subject and thus no more reality. Moreover, if we place ourselves exclusively in a perspective of justice, we no longer understand that sin opposes itself to mercy. Adam and Eve, through the prevenient mercy which they had received, were in direct contact with the Father. They had received from the Father a unique authority which absolutely no one else was to receive. However, we have difficulty accepting this: that Adam and Eve uniquely were in direct relation with God and, out of pride, destroyed the order He willed, and so God has permitted all of their descendants to be born in a fallen state.

Giving us life, creating our soul, is also an act of God's mercy. But God creates our soul in our body and we are descendants of Adam and Eve. Our living body is linked to those who are the principle, the source of the whole human race, our first parents. Consequently, because the human soul is created in the body, the mercy of the Father is limited by their rebellion. The Father's act of mercy regarding our soul has been halted by sin. In His wisdom, God permits that this be so. He could very well have done otherwise. For instance, He could have punished Adam and Eve for not having respected their authority over humanity by taking away that authority. Herein lies a mystery which we must not try to explain away, but rather highlight as mystery, with the greatest possible clarity, in order to eliminate the scandal it can arouse in us.

It is easy to eliminate the scandal once we go beyond the level of justice. If we think we can claim rights over God, we cannot understand anything. If we place ourselves before God, as having received everything from an initial act of mercy, then we understand how God, having created our soul out of mercy, allows Himself to be, as it were, vanquished, to be limited in His mercy by this initial rebellion by man. Man is responsible for original sin and God permits it. God is not responsible for it. Man impedes the act of divine mercy. God permits original sin to have all the consequences we observe, inevitable consequences given the authority God had initially given to Adam and Eve.

Second Birth: Second Act of Mercy

If we continue to reflect on these questions, we see that our own first birth has been complemented by another birth. Jesus revealed this very clearly to Nicodemus. It is important to understand the meaning of these two births. In the Old Testament we do not see it (or only very poorly). Circumcision is certainly a sign of the second birth, a sign that prefigures baptism, but it is still very distant.[25] It is in the New Testament that these two births are perfectly revealed. Now, if we no longer want to accept original sin, we no longer accept these two births. Recall the passage from John where Jesus states so emphatically to Nicodemus, "Unless one is born again of water and the Spirit, he cannot enter the Kingdom of God"... "He who is born of the flesh is flesh", that is, he belongs to the old man. "He who is born of the Spirit is Spirit", that is, he belongs to God. In us there are indeed these two births.[26]

25. See Dt 10:16; 30:6; Col 2:11-12; Gal 6:15. *ST* III q. 70, a. 1
26. See Jn 3:1-15

In other words, the first merciful act of God – that of creating and communicating life – was to be an act of substantial mercy which seizes the body, which seizes the soul, sanctifying it, making it a daughter of God. Such is the first act we see in the mystery of original justice; it is what God had wanted according to His "original will". Man failed in response to this first, plenary mercy, and God accepted. It is extraordinary that the Father, while creating the soul in a body tarnished by original sin, chooses to continue His act of mercy. The soul which he creates is born in a state of original sin. How mysterious what the mercy of God permits!

God permits it because He makes use of the sin in order to bring about something even greater: the second birth which binds us to Christ, to the new Adam, to the fullness of grace in Jesus. With the second act of the Father's mercy as regards our souls, there is something that goes farther than the first, in the qualitative order of love and mercy, for it places us in dependence, no longer upon the first Adam, the head of the human race, in the fullness of grace, but directly upon the new Adam, that is to say, upon the very source of grace. "Of His fullness we have all received."[27] We receive this fullness through baptism, the second birth in the blood of Jesus, in the grace of Jesus, which is a purely gratuitous mercy. Grace is a "quasi-substantial" mercy in the supernatural order, for although an "accident",[28] it is the principle of new life. In itself[29] it is indeed an accident, but "formally" it is, as it were, a nature,[30] that is to say, a principle of life and thus of divine filiation. Through grace we are truly sons of God. We truly possess a new "being" which binds us to Jesus and has us enter the inheritance which the Father has given to His only Son.

These two births explain the struggles between the "old man" and the life of grace. Our human psyche is initially turned towards Adam; it bathes in sin and in concupiscence. Hence, it is so complicated. God created man simple, but, through sin,

---

27. Jn 1:16
28. To use a metaphysical term: as distinguished from "substance."
29. Entitatively
30. *ST* I-II, q. 110, a. 2, a. 3

man has rendered himself manifold and complex. Our psyche has become entangled in the three concupiscences. We say "three", but it signifies a multitude. Think of all the ramifications of pride. Pride has an extraordinary "head of hair," and in every direction! Then there are the descendants of the concupiscence of life, of vanity, which are also numerous. There is an appetite, a violent concupiscence for riches which we all have within us. There is still yet the concupiscence of the flesh, something which weighs upon us. And so our psyche is "heavy" because it leans towards the "old man."

The son of God in us always risks being consigned to second place, for he was born *after* the "old man". The son of God is more naïve. Scripture shows it well: he is the "Benjamin". The son of God is beyond our psychical consciousness, for God asks him to live in faith and hence in imperfect knowledge. God demands of him to live pure love, which, in a certain sense, escapes psychial consciousness and goes much further. It leads to being "buried". With the second birth we are "buried in the death of Christ".[31]

Through the second birth, we are born into the second mercy of God of which we have been speaking. We are born in the sepulcher, in the death of Christ, and in His resurrection, therefore, in a hidden way, in possession of eternal life. Thomas Aquinas tells us that a Christian, as long as he is here on earth living in faith, is like a person with only the sense of touch. The other person, the "old man", can possess the obviousness (clarity) of human knowledge. He is like the one who sees and for whom not to see is often intolerable. He can acquire an adult personality, capable of governing himself and others. The little Benjamin on earth, the man of faith, must live in the darkness of faith, accepting to walk as if groping. He only has an experience within faith: the experience of a divine "touch," of a divine "taste." It is something very elementary as far as vision or obviousness is concerned, but infinitely profound as far as loving adherence is concerned.

---

31. See Col 2: 12; Rom 6:4

Immaculate Conception: Unique Act of Mercy

We must go still further. If we wish to understand why God allowed original sin, why Adam's sin affects all of humanity, we must look at the mystery of the Immaculate Conception. For a believer, this mystery eliminates all possible scandal concerning what God permits for the descendants of Adam and Eve. We can only discover the full meaning of this permission by God, particularly when we are troubled or scandalized, if we consider the divine plan in all its breadth. God has permitted the mystery of original sin in order to bring to realization, in an infinitely greater way, His masterpiece. God makes use of the consequences of sin in a wholly divine fashion. In and for one of the descendants of Adam and Eve, one like us, He performs a unique act of mercy, indeed, an act of mercy which takes on a whole new dimension. He performs this act for Mary in creating her immaculate in her conception.

For Mary, there was only one birth, as was the case with original justice. But there is much more than original justice here, for the one birth of Mary was a Christian birth. For each of us, the second birth comes after the first. Mary's second birth is her only birth. Everything in Mary is renewed in the grace of Christ. That is why she is so close to us, in her purity.

If the Father's act of mercy in the Immaculate Conception were only a renewal of the mystery of original justice, there would be nothing in common between the mystery of the Immaculate Conception and our grace, for we have lost original justice. We know that such a state did exist, but we have no experience of it. We can have magnificent dreams about the Garden of Eden. In fact, man has always had such dreams, for he always has a great desire for perfect human happiness. All forms of "messianism" are, as it were, desires to return to the Garden of Eden. We are constantly seeking to establish perfectly fulfilled human happiness: the perfect flourishing of our human nature in conjunction with the perfect flourishing of our divine life. We want this human flourishing to be necessary to divine flourishing and that divine flourishing perforce imply human flourishing. Very often we have such enchanting dreams. The songs of the Evil One are constantly repeating this theme, leading us to believe that, "It is surely possible, for once upon a time it did exist..." The arguments of the Devil are very forceful: "Once upon a time it existed. It is therefore possible." It is indeed possible, but it is no longer what God wants. For a dream, it suffices that it be "possible". The same holds true for seduction. In the state of original justice, there was perfect harmony between natural demands and divine demands; and each natural demand brought with it supernatural growth, each flourishing of the human heart brought forth greater love for God.

If, by this special act of the mercy of the Father towards her, Mary had been reintroduced into the Garden of Eden, the mystery of the Immaculate Conception would be far from us, and she would not be able to be our mother in the absolute sense. She would not be able, precisely because she would be in another state of grace than us.

The mystery of the Immaculate Conception is the mystery of Christian grace by which we live, perfectly realized in all its fullness. It is the new mercy of the Father. It is not something "patched up." It is a renewal of all things in and through the blood of Jesus, through the merits of Christ. It is a plenary mercy, a creative mercy which shows that Jesus has the power to recreate all things, to renew all things radically from their origin. The mercy of God the Father for this little child of His, from the moment of her conception, is *Christian mercy* similar to that which the Father gives us through baptism. Consequently, it is not something remote. It is infinitely close. It is connatural with our Christian grace. The language of the Father in His act towards Mary is not foreign to His act towards us in giving us the grace of rehabilitation which is baptism.

If we do not see this clearly then neither do we see the importance of the mystery of the Immaculate Conception for us. We may understand speculatively, but we do not understand *really*, in the perspective of God. We understand it distantly. Let us not forget that the mystery of the Immaculate Conception has been given *in order to enlighten us*. It must be a great light for us.

The mystery of the Immaculate Conception is a very great light, for it helps us to understand what the Father's mercy is, this prevenient mercy which restores all things. The Father's mercy does not just rehabilitate the prodigal son. It goes much further. It puts a stop to evil. It prevents evil from touching Mary. It takes hold of and envelops everything in Mary. This prevenient mercy of the Father for Mary is truly creative mercy, where omnipotence is entirely at the service of love in a new way. In the mystery of the Immaculate Conception we see a separation from sin. Mercy stops the contagion of evil. It prevents sin from touching and sullying the body and soul of Mary. Because of this privilege, because of the mercy of the Father which envelops everything, Mary was never sullied by sin in her human life, in her human soul, and her human body. This mercy is fatherly. Such is the extraordinary solicitude of the Father who puts a stop to the contagion of sin. And this mercy is infinitely strong. It is like a citadel in which the soul of Mary can be born, in which her little body can live.

Although first of all separation from the Fall, the Immaculate Conception is at the same time perfect harmony of the whole of human nature. All of Mary's beauty issues from this privilege. She is *all-beautiful*;[32] and there is perfect harmony. The Father recreates His masterpiece. Man did something monstrous to the masterpiece of God. He impeded the mercy of God. He prevented the Father's act from being fully expressed and consequently destroyed the work of God. The Father renews everything in divine harmony. In the fullest sense, Mary is truly and perfectly the image of God. In fact it is "necessary" because an entire generation is to come forth from her. It is necessary that she truly be first, the first of the redeemed in the

32. Cf. Song 4:7

renewal of all things. Hence everything must be harmonious in Mary. The Father's mercy establishes a full harmony between all her faculties. In her soul and body, there is no trace of anything other than the mercy of God. The words of Scripture are quite rightly attributed to the mystery of the Immaculate Conception. In her soul and in her body, "She is, as it were, the mirror that reflects the splendor of its origin."[33] In Mary, everything is absolutely pure. Everything is enveloped in mercy.

We must also state that the mystery of the Immaculate Conception implies the fullness of love, the fullness of grace. It is not enough that the image of the Father be reflected in Mary. It is necessary that Mary be the perfect receptacle of the fullness of grace, of the royal dowry which the Father gives to His little one in order to make of her His most beloved daughter. God is well pleased with this little creature, and His pleasure is expressed through an act of mercy that is totally free. The Father's choice of her is before all other choices: *elegit eam* [he chose her] and *praeelegit eam* [he chose her beforehand] (as the liturgy says). It is not sufficient to say *elegit* for, inherent in this mercy, there is, as it were, a quality in the prevenience and a unique gratuitousness. Not only did the Father put a stop to evil, not only did He will that Mary be all-beautiful, but He willed that her soul radiate with a quality of love, a quality of grace that is unique. He willed that her soul radiate a plenitude of grace from the outset which, according to certain theologians, is greater than the grace of the greatest saints at their peak. It is necessary that the seed of grace which the Father plants in Mary in His mercy initially be of greater intensity and quality than that of all the other saints.

This act of prevenient mercy helps us to understand the gratuitousness and the jealousy of the Father's love for this little child. It enables us to understand why God allowed original sin. In the Father's mind, all that preceded was permitted for the full victory of His mercy over sin, for this total and radical victory thanks to which there is not even the slightest trace of original sin in

33. Cf. Wis 7:26

Mary. In her there is nothing else but the image of the Father's mercy. There is something more beautiful in the mystery of the Immaculate Conception than in the state of original justice. There is a deep and unique orientation, a call towards the mystery of Christ.

The act of the Father's prevenient mercy is realized concretely in a very hidden way. The Father's act towards Adam and Eve in the Garden of Eden occurs before the whole world. Adam was created with grandeur and plenitude before all the angels. Indeed, the angels were in admiration of the act of the Creator who, from a little mud, fashioned His own image. For the creation of Eve, it was necessary that man himself cooperate in the masterpiece of God.

Let us consider the manner in which God has renewed all things in Mary. The Father's act of mercy is realized in a very hidden fashion, in the womb of humanity, in the womb of Mary's mother. There is not a single witness. The [good] angels understandably had knowledge of the mystery of the Immaculate Conception at the moment it took place. They were able to see its effects, that is, to perceive that this tiny child was entirely pure, unlike the others. But did they see the mystery in all of its ramifications? Did they see that the entire human race was being restored in this act of mercy?

At its very root, there is something new realized through this act. No human person had knowledge of it. God did not inform Mary's parents. Her mother must have said to herself, "I have brought into the world an absolutely delightful daughter." But she believed Mary was like other children. The mystery was reserved for God.

God buried and hid this mystery, this extraordinarily fatherly act, this unique solicitude. At the moment of Mary's conception, the whole Trinity indwelt her soul. No one on earth was aware of it. It was completely hidden. It took a very long time, in fact, before the mystery was proclaimed as a "great sign in the sky",[34] a great sign of the Father's mercy for humanity, as it

---

34. Rv 12:1

were, a sign of the renewal of all things.

Immaculate Conception: Revelation of Mercy

This mystery is revealed to us so that we might live it and not merely admire it. We know that the knowledge of faith (which receives the word of God, the revelation of God) is speculative and practical knowledge which seeks to become affective knowledge, for it implies a *pia affectio* [an inclination of the heart] and needs to be informed by charity. Each time God reveals something, it is not simply so that we admire it, but so that we contemplate it (in faith, thanks to the gifts of understanding and wisdom), that we live it as a mercy given to us.

God does not act in the somewhat cruel fashion of human beings. Human beings sometimes reveal wonderful things saying, "This is not for you." That is what today's humanity seems to be doing without realizing the cruelty of it. At Christmastime one sees children standing speechless before magnificent shop windows. For such children it is a "revelation" in a fairy tale setting. There is not only something for them to dream about, but there is enough to drive them crazy. Such children are led to think that, if they are not given what is in the shop window, then their mother and father have not understood their hearts as children. They are awe-struck and their mother is obliged to ignore it. This is one of the signs of a certain cruelty on the part of today's humanity. If humanity had more of a sense of things, this would not happen. I am convinced that such incidents have terrible consequences for children, for it awakens in them enormous desires which cannot be satisfied. Today's advertising is in line with this. We put things on display without thinking that we have no right, in the practical realm, to awaken desires which cannot be satisfied. Such is the game of seduction, the game of "shop windows."

God does not act in this way. He presents to us infinitely more than we see in shop windows. He presents a magnificent reality, something extraordinary. If He reveals to us His masterpiece in the mystery of the Immaculate Conception, He does so *for our sake*, leading us to understand that the mystery belongs to us to the extent that we believe in it, that the mystery is for us to the extent that we love it. We must live the mystery. The Father's act of prevenient mercy for His little child Mary, is for the whole Mystical Body, for those who are redeemed by Christ. We hereby understand Christian mercy, the mercy of Christ's blood, which radically redeems the sinner and completely liberates from sin. This redemption is accomplished in a different way for us and for Mary. For Mary, it occurred in a single moment. For us it occurs progressively. In heaven, we will all be immaculate. We will all live the mystery of the Immaculate Conception.

Through the mystery of Christ, God could have rendered us all immaculate right from the beginning of our life on earth. But He did not will it thus. He willed that it be, in and through Mary, that we rediscover the mystery of prevenient mercy. God willed that His mercy, in and through Mary, have a more motherly note, that it be manifested in and through the immaculate heart of Mary.

Let us not forget a principle that Thomas Aquinas gives us in his Treatise on Divine Government: what is essential in the Father's government is mercy.[35] In God, justice is absorbed by mercy.[36] It is, therefore, only with mercy that we can understand what is most proper to the Father's government in our regard. What characterizes His government, the most formal aspect of His government, is mercy. Human persons govern with justice. God governs with mercy. Always recall this principle, for very easily we project our little ideas about government on God's government. Each of us has a certain conception of human government. In the Father's government justice exists, but it is completely surpassed by mercy.

Thomas Aquinas, indeed, tells us that God likes to multiply His intermediaries, His instruments, in order to have His mercy overflow.[37] Let us apply this principle to the mystery of the Immaculate Conception. The Father renders Mary totally and

35. *ST* I q. 21, a. 3 and 4
36. *ST* I q. 21. a. 4
37. *ST* I q. 103, a. 6; *Contra Gentiles* III, ch. 77: Commentary on the Gospel of John I, no. 119

radically pure. He wills her to be the object of His mercy in an absolute and extreme fashion so that this mercy might overflow to us through her. In the beginning of the history of theology, theologians (and Thomas Aquinas himself) did not dare assert that Mary was immaculate in her conception. They said that Mary had never sinned, that she had never experienced actual sin. But the Holy Spirit has since shown us that the prevenience of the Father was even more radical in Mary. There "needed" to be not even a single trace of sin. Only the light of God is reflected in her. All of Mary's traits, both of her soul and body, are truly reflections of the Father's mercy. Everything in her is taken by this mercy — and the Father gives her to us.

The Father gives us Mary through His Son. He gives her to us at the Cross so that, in and through her, we might receive all the mercy that is in her with a note of motherly superabundance, and motherly sweetness. He gives her to us so that we might understand that everything given to her is given to us. Indeed, everything that belongs to a mother belongs to her children. This primary and radical mercy places Mary in a unique situation. She is truly the Father's little girl, essentially, initially, and entirely ordered to the Father, she "who reflects the splendor of her source, of her origin."[38] Mary is given to us so that she herself might take us in a radical fashion, so that she might bring about in us the same purification, so that, little by little, all the traits of our soul and of our body might also become a reflection of the Father's mercy.

Moses: Figure of Mary

If we wish to understand how the Father teaches us this mystery, it is good to consider its prefiguration in the Old Testament. One must never lay aside anything of God's teaching, especially when it comes to a mystery as intimate and profound as that of the Immaculate Conception. We can now

---

38. Cf Wis 7:26

question Scripture in the light of this dogma. We could not do this before the dogma was defined. As is often the case, the secrets of God are well hidden such that we cannot understand them if He does not reveal them.

The first act of the Father's mercy after the Fall is toward his servant Moses. With respect to the patriarchs, it is the goodness of God that is manifested above all, the goodness, the lovableness of the Father who binds Himself to His friends in a special covenant.

With Moses, however, we are dealing with the story of a servant. That is why I believe that Moses "prefigures" Mary. It is surprising to see how the Holy Spirit describes Moses. In choosing Moses God seems to have chosen someone, on the surface, most opposite to Mary. Moses has human grandeur, extraordinary human stature, an extremely rich temperament, close to us in many ways. With Mary we know nothing. We know nothing of Mary's psyche, for, in a certain sense, she has none. Everything in Mary is hidden in and absorbed by the Father's mercy. We can understand the temperament of Moses, however, in reading what Scripture mentions of it. Moses was visibly sculpted in granite. Michelangelo sensed it well! We see well that the physiognomy of Moses is both very human and very divine. It is very marked by the Holy Spirit, but also labored by the "old man", by his human psyche. The physiognomy of Moses is perhaps one of the most sculpted, one of the most striking in the Old Testament. Mary, however, completely escapes us. And so there is both an opposition and parallelism between Moses and Mary. The striking opposition and the parallelism must have us penetrate what is wholly divine in the intimate mystery of Mary. We must understand that, vis-à-vis Mary, the Holy Spirit wished to reveal only very hidden secrets in order to have us better penetrate them. In a certain sense, the Holy Spirit enveloped Mary exceptionally so that we might better understand both the littleness and divine grandeur of this servant of God.

Let us try to grasp through Scripture what the Holy Spirit wishes for us to understand of the mystery of the Immaculate Conception. We know that the birth of Moses is situated after the decree of Pharaoh demanding that all first born Hebrew sons be thrown into the Nile. "Each son born of a Hebrew woman must be thrown into the river; but let all the girls live."[39] We see what Pharaoh wants. He wants the destruction of all those who are to become chiefs of the people. He allows the girls to live in order to make slaves of them.

"A man of the tribe of Levi took a woman of the same lineage."[40]

It is not insignificant that it was the tribe of Levi. The tribe of Levi was not yet consecrated to God, but was eventually to be consecrated. Here we have, as it were, a sign of a prior election by God.

"This woman conceived and bore a son. Seeing how beautiful he was…"[41] *Tota pulchra est*:[42] He was like all the other children, yet totally different, so beautiful:

> Now a certain man of the house of Levi married a Levite woman, who conceived and bore a son. Seeing that he was a goodly child, she hid him for three months. When she could hide him no longer, she took a papyrus basket, daubed it with bitumen and pitch, and putting the child in it, placed it among the reeds on the river bank. His sister stationed herself at a distance to see what would happen to him.
>
> Pharaoh's daughter came down to the river to bathe, while her maids walked along the river bank. Noticing the basket among the reeds, she sent her handmaid to fetch it. On opening it, she looked, and lo, there was a baby boy, crying! She was moved with pity for him and said, "It is one of the Hebrews' children." Then his sister asked Pharaoh's daughter, "Shall I go and call one of the Hebrew women to nurse the child for you?" "Yes, do so," she

39. Ex 1:22
40. Ex 2:1
41. Ex 2:2
42. Song 4:7

answered. So the maiden went and called the child's own mother. Pharaoh's daughter said to her, "Take this child and nurse it for me, and I will repay you." The woman therefore took the child and nursed it. When the child grew, she brought him to Pharaoh's daughter, who adopted him as her son and called him Moses; for she said, "I drew him out of the water".[43]

We see the prefiguration in this text. The waters of the Nile have always been considered by the Fathers of the Church to be an image of the grip of sin. Pharaoh visibly represents the Devil. He is a "prefiguration" of the Prince of this world, of the one who desires to dominate the world, especially the children of God by throwing them into the "Nile", that is, into sin. This is the only way that he can dominate them. He thinks he has a right over all those born of the people of God, a right to bury them, to hurl them into the "Nile."

Moses should have perished like all the other children, but the mercy of God was there. Moses did nothing to be saved. He was born like all the other children, but upon him lay the mark of mercy. He is thus spared the common lot. The mercy of God is first shown in the beauty of the child Moses. The consequence of this beauty is his being placed in a small basket on the waters of the Nile to keep him from falling into them. However, this is only exterior. The Immaculate Conception is inside of Mary's soul and, through her soul, it "invades" her body. With Moses, the beauty of his body is first manifested, and then the small basket which envelops the body and keeps Moses from falling into the Nile.

There is another consequence of the prevenient act by God towards Moses. The daughter of Pharaoh is moved by all these circumstances; yet these things too remain exterior. It is the earthly life of Moses that is manifested in this prefiguration. In Mary we consider the life of her soul. Indeed, in the Father's merciful act towards the child Moses, there is a prefiguration of the Immaculate Conception. And it is good for us to try to under-

43. Ex 2:1-10

stand how the Father, how the Holy Spirit, first has us enter into this mystery and shows us this prevenient embrace of mercy.

The Father Himself keeps Mary's soul from falling into the "Nile," that is, into the contagion of sin. The Father Himself rises up in His mercy. He keeps his little child from falling into sin and being blemished by it.

It is before the power of Pharoah that the mercy of God towards Moses is manifested. It is before the power of the Devil that the mercy of God towards Mary is manifested. The mystery of the Immaculate Conception is a mystery unbearable for the Devil, for it manifests splendidly the absolute power of God over the human race. This mystery proclaims that the human race belongs to God, for the human race was created in His image. God did not forget His rights over the human race. Although men and women have abandoned God, God does not abandon them. He remains close. God manifests His closeness through this unique mercy in Mary's regard. Although she is part of the human race, a descendant of Eve like us, God envelops Mary and completely withdraws her from the influence of the Prince of this world who thinks he has rights over the human race. This right he claims is actually a permission of God, but, in his pride, he has transformed it into a right. The mystery of the Immaculate Conception reminds Satan in an absolute way that, in reality, what he thinks is a right over humanity is nothing more than a permission of God. Such aberration is always the immediate consequence of pride. Pride inflates our rights, transforming all permissions, all possibilities into rights. This is what we do in our prideful psyche. All we need to do is reflect a little to become aware of it. All of our possibilities, all that God grants, we transform, little by little, into rights. We do this in all realms, especially in the intellectual realm where pride can play a particular role.

The mystery of the Immaculate Conception shows us what radical humility is. It shows us that the Father's mercy is primary. It shows us that only his mercy can renew everything. This act of the Father in Mary's regard, the mystery of the

Immaculate Conception, teaches us in a truly masterful way what true humility is.

Immaculate Conception: Seed of Contemplation

Before this mystery, the Devil is irritated. He does not wish to be educated by the Holy Spirit. He plunges himself into pride. We, however, can still be educated by the Holy Spirit and we must do so very practically in our Christian, contemplative life. We must be educated by the mystery of the Immaculate Conception in order to understand the Father's prevenient mercy, in order to stand before the beauty of His mercy, before the beauty of Mary who totally escapes the contagion of sin to belong only to God.

According St. Bernard, who was very sensitive to this fact, admiration is at the root of our contemplative life. It is indeed true that we must maintain admiration for the Father's acts. We must also understand the practical character of this prevenient mercy which must educate us in humility and plunge us into it in order to show us that everything that is great, true and good comes from the Father's mercy. God loved us first. God does everything. When there is something good in us, it comes from God, from the Father, from His mercy. We learn true humility, contemplative, divine humility, when we understand that everything stems from mercy and that we have no "rights" which do not come from God. Such is why we can surrender everything to Him. We can give back to Him our rights. We must do this, for we are the "poor" of the Lord.

The Devil is irritated by the mystery of the Immaculate Conception, for he cannot bear such gratuitous, primal and enveloping mercy. He cannot bear the fatherhood of God. He accepts God as Creator, but he does not accept Him as Father. He tries as best as he can to reject this mystery, not to consider this mystery. He tries to diminish and give us a sort of caricature of it.

We must be careful not to fall into the Devil's trap. We must deeply and divinely exult with joy, like little children who exult in seeing the greatness of their Father's love manifested in such an act. From time to time we may lack joy regarding certain acts of the Father. But the mystery of the Immaculate Conception must be "cause of our joy", because there is no more radical act of mercy than this. We must exult with joy in this mercy, for it is given to us. We must consider this mystery as an inexhaustible source of joy. We must not let ourselves be paralyzed by our mistakes, our difficulties. We know in faith that Mary is entirely pure and that she is given to us. So there is no need for unending introspection. It is time wasted. It diminishes the mystery of the Immaculate Conception.

The Devil is no more than a "psychologist." He is the psychologist *par excellence* precisely because he wished to live only for himself. His psyche is extraordinarily lucid. It is the psyche of an angel, of a pure spirit. It is extremely penetrating, but terribly proud and entirely turned in on itself. That is why he cannot tolerate mercy, which is, as it were, the Father's great rapture. When the Father does an act of mercy, He takes hold of everything and draws it to Himself. In his proud psyche, the Devil can only accept justice. He can only accept things which are ordered according to the intellect. He cannot accept the insane gratuitousness of the Father's mercy. He asks, "Why this little child? Why is she the object of such mercy? Why her? She did nothing to merit it." It is out of pure mercy that the Father wished to take her completely to Himself. Such is the folly of God's love, the excess and the superabundance of his love, manifested to this little child whom He chose in a unique fashion.

The Father's folly, His excess of love, is for us. Mary is given to us. So let us not allow the psyche of the Devil to take hold of the psyche of the "old man" in us. Let us be careful, for the psyche of the "old man" is akin to that of the Devil. On the contrary, let blossom the divine joy in our hearts, the hearts of little children, and we will thus be conformed to the mystery of the Immaculate Conception. It is in this light that we best see

the "parting of the waters" in us: that which is connatural with
Mary and that which inclines the "old man" towards a proud
psyche like that of the Devil.

The Father's act of extravagant love is inexhaustible. It
accompanies all the mysteries of Mary in order to envelop them
with prevenient mercy. And the act remains in heaven. Because
the Father's mercy is always prevenient and thus primary, it is
never exhausted. It forever envelops. Just as motherly love
always envelops a child, even after birth, so the Father's mercy
envelops Mary in a permanent fashion, keeping her in the life-
giving warmth of His presence (*in sinu Patris*). Mary is totally
hidden in the mystery of the Father's mercy.

Immaculate Conception:
Mercy of the Father for Us

The mystery of the Immaculate Conception is given to the
entire Church militant, but it is reserved in a special way to the
contemplative life, for the contemplative life is heaven antici-
pated. The contemplative life demands that we should be
already engaged in the great mystery of heaven. Do not consider, therefore, the mystery of the Immaculate Conception as
something distant, as a magnificent spectacle. We sometimes
consider it as such. The mystery of the Immaculate Conception
is the mercy of the Father for us, engaging us very deeply in the
very mystery of His mercy and leading us to understand just
how jealously He loves us.

It is here that we see the difference between human jealousy
and divine jealousy, the jealousy of God. Each time that God
does a work of mercy with a note of unique gratuitousness, with
a note of particular jealousy, each time that God sets aside
someone He loves, it is so that all might receive this mercy.
The mercies of God are never exclusive. Our acts of love are
exclusive and jealous. That is why when we choose someone,
others are often frustrated. This is what is horrible in human
jealousy. We wish to guard and keep our "good." The mercy of

God acts in just the opposite way. With the mystery of the Immaculate Conception, Mary is totally and radically separated from the world. She is a small oasis, a "sealed fountain", a "closed garden".[44] All of these terms express the radical separation, the fatherly and divine cloister. With this mystery, God cloistered Mary. Now, each time that the Father's divine jealousy sets someone aside, each time He takes someone to Himself, each time He envelops someone in a special way, it is so that His jealous love might blossom for other persons. With God there is absolutely no exclusiveness. He takes a soul to Himself so that His mercy might superabound and overflow to others.

The mystery of the Immaculate Conception is the fruit of the Father's prevenient mercy for Mary. We must understand that this divine act belongs to us to the extent that we are children of Mary. It is for us so that we might live the same mercy, so that we might understand the Fatherly solicitude of God. Consider the strength of this text from Scripture that monks pray each evening at Compline, "He keeps watch over us like the apple of His eye."[45] Understand this as referring to the mystery of the Immaculate Conception. We must understand it as referring to each of our souls to the extent that we are enveloped by the mystery of Mary, by the mercy of the Father.

---

44. Song 4:12
45. Ps 16:8

Mary, Mystery of Mercy

2

Presentation of Mary

Presentation of Mary

The second act of the Father's prevenient[46] mercy as regards Mary is manifested in the presentation of Mary in the Temple. It is interesting to consider the particular physiognomy of the Father's different acts of mercy, for, through them, we enter into his mystery in a special way.

The Father's mercy is not only prevenient. By definition an excess of love, it is necessarily radical and creative. When God says that we must build "upon the rock,"[47] is he not teaching us that we must build upon mercy? Acts of the Father's mercy which envelop and renew everything are the "rock".

In and through this prevenient mercy, the Father wishes to educate his children. Prevenient mercy is the creative omnipotence of God at the service of love. We must, therefore, see blossom in this mercy other acts which lead to a deeper, more secret, more intimate reality: the mystery of the Father's love manifested towards his little child, Mary. The Father educates his child to teach her how to love. In mercy He wants Mary to cooperate in an efficacious and personal fashion, for she must not simply remain one who has been enveloped. She must not remain like the child Moses, who was entirely passive. Moses cried in his basket for he was still of the Old Testament. Mary must be enveloped in a unique and complete fashion, which is divine and fatherly. And in such enveloping, the little child must respond. This response to mercy is yet again a mercy, for we can do nothing without mercy.

Presentation: Consecration to the Father

Let us try to understand Mary's response to this first act of the Father's mercy. This response is transmitted to us by Tradition.

---

46. *ST* I-II q. 3, a. 3; Ps 58:11 *Misericordia ejus praeveniet me*
47. Cf. Mt 7:24-25; Lk 6:48

The Mystery of the Immaculate Conception is indeed hidden in Scripture. There are several distant prefigurations of it. I mentioned that of Moses, for, in a certain way, it is the prefiguration which most strikes our imagination.[48] We could also mention those underscored in *Ineffabilis Deus*,[49] that of the enmity between the woman and the serpent[50] and the vision of the Woman in the Book of Revelation.[51] These are also prefigurations, although negative, of the struggle between Mary and the Devil.

Scripture says very little of what Tradition calls the mystery of the Presentation of Mary in the Temple. At the Annunciation,[52] Mary's response to the angel, and her attitude, show that she is totally consecrated to God. The passage is unintelligible if it is not understood in this way. There is a fact revealed here, indirectly, in a very hidden fashion. Mary responds to the angel, "How can this be, for I have no husband?" And yet, it is previously said that Mary is "betrothed to Joseph." Herein lies a mystery. If we place these two passages in parallel in a material, literal fashion, they are incomprehensible. They, in fact, prove that there is a secret between Mary and God: Mary has consecrated her whole being to God. This total consecration is Mary's first response to the Father's prevenient mercy, to the mercy of the Immaculate Conception.

The only way for a creature to present itself to God is to consecrate itself to God. Enveloped by the Father's mercy, Mary can only present herself to Him by consecrating herself totally, body and soul. Such is the mystery of virginity in its most powerful and deepest sense. Virginity is consecration to God of

---

48. Ex 2:1-10; St. Thomas, speaking of Mary's sanctification from her mother's womb, recalls the sanctification of Jeremiah (Jer 1:5) and John the Baptist (Lk 1:15). Cf. *ST* III, q. 27, a.1.
49. Papal Bull, December 8, 1954
50. Gn 3:15
51. Rv 12 and the various affirmations from Song: 2:2; 3:6; 4:1, 7:12, 5:2; 6:9; the text from Prv 8:22; 9:1
52. Lk 1:26-38

one's whole being, consecration to His service, total reservation for Him, total offering and gift to Him.[53] Such is the first total cooperation of a little "creature," of a child of God, entirely enveloped by the Father's mercy, who experiences this mercy, and in experiencing it, responds by totally consecrating itself. Consecration springs from the encounter of a creature, enveloped by mercy, with its God, with its Father.

Consecration binds us to the mystery of the Father. It ought to have us enter into the solitude of God. It is therefore perfectly normal that it be the only way to present oneself to God. To present oneself to God is to stand face-to-face with Him, to stand before Him. But how can a poor little creature stand before God? If the creature is entirely borne by the Father's mercy, entirely seized by the Father's mercy, it can then stand before him: it can do so only by leaning upon this mercy. That is why, in professing vows, a religious beseeches the mercy of God. It is not insignificant. It is in fact the adequate, appropriate response. It is not only because we are sinners that we beseech the mercy of God. There is more. We beseech the mercy of God because we cannot consecrate ourselves to God without leaning wholly upon his mercy. The poor little creature can only present itself to God by leaning completely upon His mercy. We cannot stand before God unless we are filled with this fatherly mercy, such that there be only the face of the Father in us, that is, His mercy. God can only look at His image, and there is the image of God in us only to the extent that we are entirely renewed in mercy, only to the extent that the Father's Christian mercy recreates us.

It is therefore perfectly normal that the first cooperation, the first response of Mary, kept by Tradition, be her "virginal consecration." The other vows come later.

It is interesting to note the difference between Mary's consecration and the (Dominican) religious consecration made through the vow of obedience. The latter is very formal because the Dominicans are an order of theologians. Only the essential

---

53. Cf. *ST* I-II, q. 186, a. 1: "Those are called religious who give themselves up entirely to the divine service, offering themselves to God as a holocaust."

element is indicated; the rest is implied. Mary's consecration, as scripture manifests it, is a virginal consecration. It is important to understand the difference. For us, an official consecration made through vows is a consecration in the Church. It pre-supposes God's call and implies a first, intimate response which is already a consecration. The official consecration in the community of the Church, made according to a deter-mined rite, hides the secret of virginal consecration of body and soul. Obedience alone reveals the official, communitari-an aspect which veils the intimate secret.

Virginal consecration is joyous. Mary responded, exultant with joy. There is nothing more joyous than to experience divinely the Father's mercy and to live by it. There is nothing more joyous than to understand that such mercy is a fatherly embrace which takes possession of His little child to introduce and hide her in His mystery in a unique way. Virginal consecration is indeed the embrace of the Father, who takes full possession of His little child. That is why this consecration is made with joy and is hidden. Consecration through the vow of obedience, on the other hand, is made *coram populo*, that is, in front of everyone. There need to be witnesses. The virginal consecration of Mary took place in a secret, intimate fashion, so much so, that Scripture does not speak of it explicitly. "He who has an ear, let him hear."[54]

The Church later affirmed the consecration of Mary. We do not have the right to consider it as something secondary. In a cer-tain sense, the Church begins with it. The Father envelops Mary in His mercy and in so doing, envelops His Church. In the end, in heaven, the whole Church will be gathered in this mercy. That is why it is said that "He will dwell with them, and they shall be His people, and God Himself shall be with them, and be their God,"[55] all will be given to the Father.[56] We will all be enveloped by the mystery of God. The mystery of the Immaculate Conception is the great embrace of the Father, but the Church does not begin here. The fundamental element of the Church, that upon which the Church is organized, is this mystery of virginal

54. Rv 2:29
55. Rv 21:3
56. Jn 6:37-40, Jn 17:12, 24, 1 Cor 12:24, Cf. Preface of the Feast of Christ the King

consecration. It is in this consecration that Mary cooperates, in an efficacious and primary fashion, with the mercy of the Father. Scripture communicates this mystery to us, all the while veiling it.

If we remove or strip away the legendary elements of what is transmitted in the Tradition, we are obliged to say that we do not know very much about the Presentation of Mary. In fact, we only know that it took place, as the liturgy keeps it.[57] Tradition shows us the mystery of the Presentation as the first act of the Virgin Mary's life, but we do not know how it occurred, or what age Mary was. Painters have tried to depict the scene. Such representations can help our devotion, but they are not the mystery itself. Our faith must seek to be pure. Our faith must lean only upon the word of God, upon what is directly revealed. Faith always seeks to distinguish the mystery itself from mere reflections of it. Now what Tradition keeps, once sifted from legend, is revealed directly by God. If we consider the mystery of the Presentation through Tradition, we notice that Tradition has only kept the mystery. Mary gave herself, presented herself to God. Tradition reveals to us the simple fact, so that we might understand that the first act of Mary, upon divinely experiencing who the Father is for her, is to present herself immediately in the Temple, to give and surrender herself completely to God.

Theologians have tried to study Mary's vow. St. Albert the Great[58] says that Mary was able to make this vow only because she was moved by the Holy Spirit, *solo inspirante Spiritu Sancto*, without asking advice from other persons. Mary did not ask advice from other persons, for it was the Holy Spirit guiding her. If she had asked advice from the Levitical priests, they would not have understood anything. They only understood what was demanded by the law. They would have told her to marry, for she

---

57. "Lord God, you wanted the Blessed Virgin Mary, sanctuary of the Holy Spirit, to be presented in the Temple on this day. Grant us through her intercession, the grace of being able to be presented to you one day in the temple of your glory." Prayer for the feast of November 21. Regarding legendary elements, see the Protoevangelium of James, apocrypha from the middle of the second century, which claims to provide what is missing from the canonical gospels about Mary's life. Cf. E. Amann, *Le Protevangile de Jacques*, Letouzey 1910.

58. Dominican Friar, Doctor of the Church teacher of St. Thomas Aquinas, 1206-1280.

was a descendent of David, and from David was to come the Messiah. In the mystery of Mary's consecration, there is something which escapes the structure of the Old Testament, something which is already of the New Testament, something which is, as it were, the dawn of the evangelical law. The demand of this vow, in its most intimate aspect, escapes the control and the jurisdiction of the Old Testament. That is why it could only be made in the light of the Holy Spirit, and under His guidance.

There is something extraordinary here: this wholly divine reality, the mystery of Mary's presentation, completely escapes the exterior, official aspect of the people of Israel. The mystery of the Immaculate Conception was hidden in the womb of Mary's mother. The mystery of the Presentation is hidden in the heart of Tradition. The womb of Mary's mother represents humanity. It was necessary that that the Father renew all of humanity at its very source. As soon as Mary responds to God, consecrating herself to him, it is necessary that this be within the inmost mystery of Tradition. From a human viewpoint, tradition is nothing other than the richness and the culture of a group. The tradition of a family, for example, is the accumulation of human values kept from generation to generation. From a religious and supernatural viewpoint, the people of Israel, the chosen people, progressively acquired a certain tradition comprised of human religious values, as well as divine values, to the extent they lived by the word of God. Christian Tradition begins with the mystery of the Presentation. That is why Mary, and religious life, are linked to Tradition. Tradition is nothing other than the cooperation of the faithful, of the members of Christ with the Holy Spirit. It is the mystery of the word of God lived in the saints. It is the breath of the Holy Spirit taking possession of the hearts of the saints to have them live the mystery of the word of God. Indeed, Tradition begins in the heart of Mary with this first response. Here also lies the mystery of consecration through religious vows.

It is sometimes said, "Religious vows are not in Scripture, they are an invention of the Church." Indeed, they are an invention of the Church, the Church in its greatest aspect! They are an invention of the Holy Spirit in the heart of Mary. It is true that if we eliminate the mystery of Mary, it is very difficult to understand religious vows.

As previously stated, Mary most certainly made this first vow under the inspiration of the Holy Spirit without human advice. Consequently, as Cajetan[59] says, in the footsteps of Thomas Aquinas, she could only make it "conditionally."[60] This must not be understood literally; one does not place conditions on the Holy Spirit. When the Holy Spirit moves us to do something and we say, "Ah, yes, but, but …" it is not a good thing. In so doing, we place restrictions. The "condition" that Thomas Aquinas notes is not a restriction. It simply shows the formal aspect of the vow. Mary could not ask advice from anyone and her vow was necessarily to lead to a particular way of life. From a human viewpoint, the vows lead to particular *mores*, to a particular environment for life. There are particular religious traditions due to the fact that a religious is entirely given to God. Unable to ask advice from anyone, Mary abandoned herself to the sole guidance of the Holy Spirit: "If this is God's good will and pleasure." She consecrated herself to God, surrendering herself completely to His "good will and pleasure" for her. The most formal aspect of the consecration is this entrusting to God which leads to dispossession of self, and belonging only to His loving will, in order to be his little child, placed in His hands.

Consecration and the Mystery of Abandonment

Thomas Aquinas's remark helps us to understand the mysterious foundation of Mary's consecration. Her consecration implies a mystery of abandonment. The "condition" of which Thomas Aquinas speaks shows us that Mary, in consecrating herself, surrenders and abandons herself totally to the "good-will and pleasure" of God.

We must understand the connection between consecration and abandonment. On the one hand, consecration demands a certain abandonment; and the more perfect the consecration, the more perfect the abandonment must be. On the other hand, true abandon-

59. Cajetan, Tommaso de Vio, Thomistic theologian and writer, 1469-1534.
60. *ST* III, q. 28, a. 4. ad. 1. Leonine Editions Commentary Number 2: *Virginitatem vovit … sub conditione, si Deo placeret*

ment calls for consecration and prepares for it. This is important to understand, for we thereby grasp how the mystery of the Presentation of Mary must be lived by all Christians, not only those who make an "official" religious profession.

For all Christians, abandonment is a fundamental, evangelical demand, a disposition to interior consecration. The mystery of abandonment must be present in the life of all Christians as the first effect of Mary's motherly mercy. Everyone can live abandonment, no matter what the circumstances may be, and, in living abandonment, one lives what is most fundamental in the evangelical law. It can even be said that abandonment allows one to live fully the spirit of virginal consecration. Only abandonment can give divine meaning to the religious life and to virginal consecration.

When Mary, moved by the Holy Spirit, consecrated herself totally to God, she did so as an act of response to all the Father's mercy towards her. In a certain sense, the act was the engagement of all of God's gifts. It was the most divinely adequate response to the grace given by God. She entrusted herself completely to God in order to belong only to Him, so that everything in her would be entirely hidden in His will. Such is the mystery of the virginity of Mary's soul and body: everything in her was surrendered to God so that He alone can make use of her according to His "good will and pleasure." Mary presented herself to the mercy of the Father through the mystery of her total consecration, a consecration that is realized in perfect abandonment.

In the eyes of God, the virginal consecration of Mary was, as it were, the most marvelous fruit of her abandonment to His mercy. The consecration was rooted in abandonment and allowed the abandonment to be exercised fully, with no restrictions. Hence we can say that the mystery of abandonment expresses the foundation and the spirit of Mary's vow of virginity, as well as what is most hidden in this vow, its most radical aspect. In the light of God's wisdom, what gave this vow all of its depth and fullness is the fact that it was made in complete abandonment. Is this vow not precisely the most perfect way for a creature to respond to the prevenient mercy of God? Would not any other way of responding to the Lord's call have been, as it were, a reduction of the mercy? Virginal consecration, realized in total abandonment, is indeed the most perfect response to God from a creature elevated by God to the supernatural order, from a human being entirely renewed by grace.

The first response of the creature to God, after having been banished from the Garden of Eden, as Scripture transmits it, is the act of the first sons of humanity. Cain and Abel address God in an act of adoration, an act of oblation of the goods of this world. Cain offers the fruits of the earth. Abel offers the first fruits of his flock.[61] If we examine from a metaphysical viewpoint the fundamental attitude of the creature as it presents itself to God, we observe that it can only do so in an act of adoration. For the creature *per se*, the only true attitude before the Creator is that of complete self-effacement. Adoration is an act of the virtue of religion in its perfection, in its plenitude. In adoration, the creature places itself in all truthfulness, as creature, before its Creator. It adores the Creator and thus effaces itself before Him.[62] An act of adoration implies that we burn and annihilate the victim. Such is a complete act of holocaust. The act performed spontaneously by Cain and Abel shows us the first act of the creature as such before its Creator.

In Mary, however, we must not consider only her dependence as creature upon God. She is indeed a child of Eve, but she is also a beloved child of God. A child of God is one who lives in faith, hope, and love. What is the spontaneous attitude of a child toward its father? Love. Faith and hope are entirely ordered to love, to charity, to enable charity to be truly a friendship with God, a friendship which must grow, which must take hold of our whole life. It is to this end that faith and hope tend.[63]

The spontaneous act of a child of God is therefore that of loving its Father. Yet, because the child is also a creature, the act

---

61. See Gn 4:3-4
62. See *ST* II-II, q. 84, a. 1
63. *ST* II-II, q. 23, a. 6

of adoration and the act of love must be combined into a single act: precisely that of abandonment.

If we analyze abandonment from a theological viewpoint, we see that it demands love. To abandon oneself truly, one must have complete trust in the superabundant love of the Father and consider only this excessive love. Abandoning oneself consists in leaning entirely upon the mercy of the Father and having nothing else upon which to lean. Abandonment requires a sense of the Father's mercy, of this immense mercy, which is an abyss of superabundant, excessive love that surpasses everything we can experience. A divine sense of mercy stems from living faith and from hope. Does not living faith have us discover what is most intimate in the mystery of God, that is, His tireless and faithful mercy? Does not hope lean upon the merciful omnipotence of the Father?[64]

However, the child of God is also a creature. Hence this love which leans entirely upon divine omnipotence, humbles the creature and leads it to consider itself as nothing before God. This love moves the creature to surrender itself totally to the "good will and pleasure" of God, so that God might do what He will. Abandonment requires such an attitude. It requires that there be no care or worry regarding human goods. All natural avidity and "overly human" pursuits must disappear, yielding to God's will alone. This requires a very interior act of holocaust, a holocaust of the will, of one's own judgement, a holocaust of all that is grand in human life, of all human aspiration. Without this holocaust, there can be no abandonment. Such a holocaust, however, must be entirely burned by love. It is not just the simple act of adoration of a creature, but an act of adoration entirely transformed by faith, hope and love. It is therefore adoration become entirely interior.

In its deepest sense, abandonment is the union of adoration with love which leads to complete self-effacement before the inexhaustible mercy of the Father; or, better said, which leads to throwing oneself into [divine] mercy so that mercy might

---

64. *ST* II-II, q. 17, a. 1

take hold of everything, take possession of the vital strength of one's being. Through abandonment, we desire that mercy be exercised as perfectly as possible upon our whole person. That is why we offer to God's mercy all that we can: our faculties, our development, everything in us that is to grow and blossom. All of these things we surrender to the mercy of the Father so that it might penetrate our inmost life.

We thus understand that abandonment is the only adequate act with respect to the Father's prevenient mercy. All other acts diminish this mercy by seeking to posses it, by reducing it to what we ourselves understand or hope it might be. We all do this instinctively. In order to eliminate any possessiveness, in order to leave the Father entirely free, there needs be the spontaneous act of a beloved child of the Father. The act is that of abandoning self as deeply and as perfectly as possible.

Consecration is, therefore, only fully consecration in abandonment. Consecration which is only a concern for the personal perfection of virtue is a sort of Pharisaism. Alas, in the religious life there is always a possibility for such Pharisaism or human "stylishness" in the heart of consecration itself. With such an attitude we risk considering ourselves better than others because we have consecrated ourselves to God. This leads to human contentment which goes directly against the spirit of consecration, and the mystery of abandonment. When a certain possessiveness surfaces in religious consecration it tarnishes that which should be luminous with the very light of God. If we want to be pure and consecrated in our own eyes, by ourselves, we tarnish that which must shine with no other light than that of God. Religious vows can only be true to the extent they are presently lived in abandonment. Otherwise, we fall into Pharisaism. Saint Augustine sensed the possibility for pride in religious consecration[65], the possibility for human conceit, the temptation to consider oneself more perfect because called by God. Regarding this he says, "If a virgin boasts in her virginity, she is less than a 'simple' Christian woman humbly living her Christian life. " God wants

---

65. *De Sancte Virginitatem*, XXXI sq.

at all costs to eliminate pride from our lives. For that, it suffices for us to return to the very origin of our vows, that is, Mary's act of abandonment. Our consecration to God is authentically divine only to the extent it is based on abandonment. Again, abandonment is the adequate response to the Father's mercy. Let us try to penetrate this important mystery even more, for it alone allows us to avoid Pharisaism, to avoid blinders, to avoid placing limitations on the mercy of God.

Our abandonment must take on the form of spontaneous, childlike abandonment, in the evangelical sense. It is truly the abandonment of children that can enable us to grasp divine abandonment. This is the only way that we abandon ourselves perfectly: like a little child in its mother's arms. The child has no other support than these motherly arms. It surrenders itself, for it is secure, for it knows that its mother will not abandon it. This it senses instinctively. In other arms the child would be restless: it would cry. Once it finds itself in the arms of its mother again, it can relax, to the point of complete abandonment in sleep. The sleep of a child is the most adequate image to represent divine abandonment in our souls; but it is only an *image*.

Divine abandonment consists in leaning only upon the "arms" of the Father, upon the merciful omnipotence of the Father which envelops us. It consists in allowing ourselves to be carried by this mercy, in allowing ourselves to be "invaded" by it in our inmost selves. We must open the doors of our soul, allowing it to be filled with divine mercy. We must allow the mercy of the Father to be our only support so that we truly experience divine abandonment. Such is the *sine qua non* condition for silent, interior prayer (*oraison*): such is the foundation of the Christian life. Divine abandonment is complete passivity in an act of faith, hope, and love. It is the receptivity of our being to the Father's mercy, which surpasses all that we can understand, and which envelops us. When our only concern is the mercy of the Father, when we abandon ourselves with total trust like a child in the arms of its mother, our soul experiences great divine "relaxation", divine "sleep".

We must be careful, however, not to confuse abandonment with psychical sluggishness which translates into inactivity and indetermination. Being abandoned does not mean being apathetic. Being abandoned does not mean having no character or stature. Idleness and psychical laziness can exist under the pretense of abandonment. This is not abandonment. Abandonment is extremely "determined." It penetrates and takes possession of our being from its pinnacle. In abandonment our being is engaged in its deepest and most noble aspect, and given to the service of the Father's mercy. The "old man" then becomes a servant and accepts not to determine himself, but rather to be entirely docile to what God wills and to await God's determination.[66]

Abandonment demands surrender to divine mercy, considering that divine mercy alone can render our activities efficacious.[67] Abandonment implies understanding that doing our work in dependence upon God, and acting only in the light of God has eternal value. Everything outside of the light of God, the will of God, and the mercy of God is grass that withers, grass that exists only for a time.[68] The excesses in our life, that is, everything outside the will and mercy of the Father, do not really exist. They are grass to be burned[69]. Everything outside of God, everything not in the light of mercy, is vain. It is this clear perspective which enables us to abandon ourselves.

Such statements as, "Do not worry for your lives, for what you will eat: consider the birds of the sky,"[70] show us just how evangelical abandonment is. Jesus' primary teaching (especially in the Synoptic gospels), concerns abandonment. This is understandable, for Jesus finds himself before persons who love earthly riches and cling to them. Jesus taught the Jews that it is not possible to follow Him and to receive the Good News, without abandon-

---

66. It is also necessary to note that although this attitude of abandonment implies a surpassing of the rational mode of prudence, it is in no way a suppression of prudence: what comes from God is eminently prudent. Abandoning oneself to God's omnipotence is sovereignly prudent. The greatest act of imprudence is to be lacking in abandonment.
67. See Jn 15:5
68. Cf. Is 40:7 & 8; Ps 90:5-6
69. Jn 15:6
70. Mt 6:25-34

ment. Jesus says it in a particularly poetic fashion, for abandonment lends itself to such expression. Jesus speaks of the flowers of the field. He shows us the field adorned, magnificent, with incomparable richness, richness which no one else possesses, precisely because it is from the Father. The flowers of the field and the birds of the air receive all benefits from the Father. How would it then be for a person who truly abandons himself? If he could truly abandon himself, he would receive infinitely more than he can acquire by himself, for he lets himself be carried by the One who wishes to be his only Father, full of mercy, who loves him more than he loves himself.

Evangelical littleness entails more than abandonment, but abandonment is its primary characteristic;[71] abandonment is its foundation stone. Abandonment is, as it were, the alpha and the omega of the Christian life, the fundamental attitude of the Christian life.

When we disregard abandonment, we disregard the true gospel attitude: we disregard mercy. We are thus impoverished and become like ships that have lost what enables them to stay on course. Abandonment means stability for us. When we disregard abandonment, even in the slightest way, we begin to experience anxiety. Abandonment is the only true way to overcome anxiety. That is why Jesus asks it of us in a particular way. He knows that anxiety is one of the evils of our time. We are all tense and stressed. The only way to eliminate anxiety from our lives is to live in abandonment more and more. It does not necessarily eliminate all psychical anxiety immediately. But in the depths of who we are, there is a surrender to the will of God. We must dominate anxiety, which comes from the "old man" who is hard-pressed because the Son of Man is perhaps soon to come. The old man fears the Second Coming and is anxious. We must surpass the old man, not by fighting him directly, but by dominating anxiety through abandonment and total surrender to the Father's mercy. For this we must forbid ourselves all judgement, for once we begin to judge, we fall to the level of the anxious person in us.

---

71. Cf. pp. 76 sq.

We must succeed in surrendering everything to the Father's mercy, in opening our hearts to this mercy. What we really understand about our lives and those of others is very little. When we establish ourselves as capable of understanding, even somewhat, how God leads us, we diminish God's fatherly guidance.

It is good to recognize the graces that God has given, but let it be in abandonment, without seeking to reduce them to our judgement. When we consider our faults let it be in abandonment to Him who forgives, and who uses our faults for something greater. If we claim that our faults are irremediable, that our life is a failure, we place ourselves outside of abandonment. We then fall into the anxiety characteristic of our age. Anxiety is the "enfant terrible" of our age. This we recognize and seek to remedy by offering our lives all the more in abandonment to the Father's mercy. Let us surrender to Him beforehand all that is to come, with no judgement of our own. This is the evangelical attitude that is deepest and most necessary in our life.

The first words that Jesus said when coming into this world were *Ecce venio*: "Sacrifice or oblation you wished not, but ears open to obedience you gave me. Holocausts or sin offerings you sought not. Then said I, 'Behold, I come. In the written scroll it is prescribed for me to do your will.' "[72] Purely "material" adoration does not suffice for God. The consecration of material things, even important ones, does not suffice. Such consecration is still the immolation of "sacrifices" and "victims", of "rams and bullocks."[73] What God wants is a contrite, loving, and abandoned heart, given entirely to His mercy.[74] This is the meaning of the first *Ecce venio* of Christ. Mary understood it and she prepared for it. Is not Mary the dawn of the evangelical life? Before Jesus ever said it, the Holy Spirit prepared this *Ecce venio* in Mary's heart.

The last words of Jesus on the cross, *In manus tuas*[75], are also the absolute surrender of everything into the hands of the Father. They are also abandonment, although sorrowful aban-

72. Heb 10:5-7 (Ps 40:7-9)
73. Cf. Is 1:11-13: "In the blood of bulls and goats I find no pleasure." "I do not delight in the blood of bulls and goats."
74. Cf. Ps 51:18-19; Ps 50:8-15; Ps 34:19
75. "Father, into your hands I commend my spirit" Cf. Lk 23:46 and Ps 31:6

donment in apparent defeat and failure. If, upon the Cross, Jesus had begun to judge what was happening from a human viewpoint, He would have fallen into despair or at least horrible anxiety. There needed to be total surrender into the hands of the Father, fully conscious of all that was happening, without hiding any of it. Jesus saw the apparent failure of the Cross. He saw that His whole body was racked. But it was not important. His soul was entirely in the hands of the Father. From the Cross He said again, "You do not want the blood of rams and bullocks. You gave me a will capable of loving, capable of abandoning completely to Your will and Your mercy."

Mary said nothing different than that. In the mystery of her Dormition she said nothing other than that. She presented herself to God in an act of complete and absolute abandonment. Everything began and ended in an *In manus tuas*.

Whenever we feel agitated, apprehensive, or fearful, we must readopt this attitude, the only true attitude. All others are not evangelical. This is what Mary teaches us. This attitude is even more true in the religious life where Pharisaism is always tempting. There is a risk of wanting only to lean upon the law, upon the grandeur and nobility of the religious life. The only true support, the only rock, is abandonment to the Father's mercy.

Abandonment is also the only way to escape temptations from the Devil. When we abandon ourselves we are completely hidden from the Devil. When Mary abandoned herself to the Father's will, the Father took possession of everything in her. She knew in her heart that in abandoning herself in this way she was going to the "desert" of the Father's mercy.[76] When we do an act of abandonment, we escape the pursuit of the Devil. He can no longer follow us. He has no trace of us, for he is unfamiliar with the mercy of God. He fears and hates the mercy of God. He does not come near it. If, in abandonment, we truly let ourselves be enveloped, if we let the mercy of the Father take hold of everything in us, we truly become "the mercy of the Father" and the Devil can no longer harm us. We escape him.

76. See Rv. 12:6

Obviously, our acts of abandonment are never complete. The "old man" in us has such difficulty abandoning himself and letting himself be embraced. But to the extent our abandonment is complete, especially to the extent our abandonment is with Mary, we escape the Devil. Mary is given to us for this. Mary is given to us so that we might live her mystery. We can only fully live the mystery of evangelical abandonment with her and through her. And in so doing we become an enigma for the Devil. This is the only way to escape him completely. If we proceed otherwise, in any way whatsoever, we cannot escape him totally. The moment we begin to reflect upon what we might be able to do, the moment we begin to evaluate, to judge and to see all that is in our power, placing ourselves in a psychological perspective, we place ourselves in a perspective that the Devil knows much better than us. He knows better the psychical contours of the "old man." To escape the power of the Devil we must go beyond such trust in self, trust founded exclusively on our own consciousness, on ourselves, and throw ourselves into mercy.

From Moses to Mary: From the Servant to the Child of God

In order to understand the greatness of Mary's act, it is also necessary to consider its prefiguration. This prefiguration sheds light, for it is very close to what we ourselves often do, and considered in contrast to Mary's act, it helps us to understand the greatness of the latter.

We must consider in the Old Testament Moses' response to the Father's prevenient mercy and compare it to that of Mary. The first act of Moses that Scripture transmits to us is an act of justice. Indeed, Moses accomplishes three successive acts of justice.[77]

On one occasion after Moses had grown, [Mary was a little child... there is an extraordinary contrast here] when he visited his kinsmen and witnessed their forced labor, he saw an Egyptian striking a Hebrew, one of his own kinsmen. Looking about and seeing no one, he slew the

---

77. Ex 2:11-17

Egyptian and hid him in the sand.

The next day he went again and now two Hebrews were fighting! So he asked the culprit, 'Why are you striking your fellow Hebrew?' But he replied, 'Who has appointed you ruler and judge over us? Are you thinking of killing me as you killed the Egyptian?' Then Moses became afraid and thought the affair must certainly be known.

Pharaoh too heard of the affair and sought to put him to death, but Moses fled from him and stayed in the land of Midian.

As he was seated there by a well, seven daughters of a priest of Midian came to draw water and fill the troughs to water their father's flock. But some shepherds came and drove them away. Then Moses ran and defended them and watered their flock.

Behold three acts of vindictive justice. If we have a sense of justice and find ourselves before something unjust, we side with the one suffering unjustly. Moses does this in a royal, extraordinary fashion.

It is very interesting to observe, because the psyche of Moses is shown to us here. Moses is a fiery, spirited, rather irascible, and, at the same time, timid man. And as it often occurs with timid persons, he cannot contain himself. Scripture tells us expressly, "Moses himself was by far the gentlest man on the face of the earth."[78]

Notice how God prepared Moses, how God trained Moses. Even when irascibility in us is very strong and we are capable of an act like that of Moses, God wishes to make of us gentle, meek servants. God deeply transforms the "matter" of the old man. What we observe clearly in Moses is the "matter" of the old man. And so the first act of vindictive justice is Moses killing the Egyptian and burying him in the sand.

The second act of vindictive justice is Moses as judge between two Hebrew brethren who are fighting. This is also

---

78. Nm 12:3 *Erat enim Moyses vir mitissimus super omnes homines.*

justice whose act is more elevated.

The third act of vindictive justice is Moses reestablishing justice. The seven daughters of the priest of Midian had arrived first to the well and had their flocks drinking when shepherds arrive and drive them away. Moses becomes irritated. He immediately defends these foreign women. He did not know them, but he had a sense of justice.

I find all of this very significant for us. Moses responds to mercy with justice. This is what we automatically do when our heart is at least somewhat noble. It is the response of a servant who is but a servant. It is the response of the old man who has not yet become a child of God. It is the response of everything in us that is connatural to us. Justice is noble and great. And to the mercy of the Father, Moses responds with justice.

We easily respond to the Father's prevenient mercy with justice instead of abandonment. Consequently, we limit the Father's mercy. Our response is not adequate to this mercy. There is an abyss between abandonment and justice. In abandonment, we open ourselves to another mercy and we recognize that mercy is everything. In abandonment, we seek to make ourselves fully docile, and divinely receptive to this mercy. When we respond with justice, we respond according to our own judgement, according to our way of receiving God's love.

Moses received mercy in a very beautiful and grand fashion. He responded by becoming the defender of his brethren. It was very noble, but insufficient. There is an abyss between Mary and Moses. Moses' three acts of mercy show us a perfectly conscious response which is grand and noble, but which remains that of a servant and is not that of a child.

We immediately see the consequences: in responding with justice, Moses leans upon his own virtue. He indeed testifies to great prudence: he looks around before killing the Egyptian. Yet, despite his prudence and his justice, he does not experience peace. The next day, after another act of justice, he begins to fear. He is afraid and says, "The affair must certainly be known." He withdraws into himself. When he killed the Egyptian, Moses showed a certain nobility. He showed that he was capable of cleanly accomplishing a rather noble act. But then he loses his footing, which is very significant.

When we respond to the mercy of God only with virtue (prudence, justice) we reduce the mercy of God to our size, to our dimension. Reducing the mercy of God to our size, is to lean only upon our own virtue. In so doing, we no longer have the divine strength which the mercy of God gives. The only way to avoid all fear and all human anxiety is precisely to lean only upon the mercy of God, to respond to mercy with an act of complete abandonment, to open ourselves completely to mercy according to the divine good will and pleasure. All other ways of responding leave possibilities for fear. We will never be prudent enough or just enough. If we remain only focused on ourselves, there will always be room for anxiety and fear which paralyze, which impede us from progressing. In such cases, what is missing is a divine response to mercy in abandonment.

We can also use this prefiguration in another way. Between Moses and Mary the contrast is very clear. We ourselves are somewhat between the two. In us there is something very close to Moses and in us there is something very close to Mary.

Moses is very close to the psyche of the "old man." He was educated in the school of Pharaoh. He was indeed the object of God's mercy, but he lived with Pharaoh. And Pharaoh represents human efficiency. Pharaoh represents a humanistic viewpoint. From this viewpoint, Moses has a psyche very close to that of the "old man" in each one of us. Moses was blessed by God. Moses was transformed by God, but he was yet to have the psyche of a friend of God. He had the psyche of someone in the house of Pharaoh whose *mores* he shared.

In each one of us there is something very close to Moses and something whereby we understand that we must go further. The Old Testament cannot serve as a model for us. It simply sheds some light on the mystery of Mary and the mystery of Christ. Here it sheds some light on the presentation of Mary in the tem-

ple. If Moses has something close to us, we must make use of
what he does. He kills an Egyptian. This is very important for
abandonment. We must kill the "Egyptian." The Egyptian is the
from the school of Pharaoh, one whose sole aim is efficiency.
The Egyptian is one who wishes to respond only with personal
initiatives, who wishes to "accomplish something," who wishes to build pyramids. We all have a desire to build "pyramids,"
to build enormous structures. We often wish to make of our
Christian life something that defies time, something that defies
other persons, something perfect. Such is the desire of the
Egyptian. It is not insignificant that Egypt is one of the greatest
human civilizations. Is not Egypt, as it were, the synthesis of
the greatest riches and the greatest human knowledge? In order
to abandon ourselves, we must eliminate false appetites for
grandeur, the appetites in us only to build "pyramids."

Abandonment is not an attitude of carelessness. Abandonment
is not the attitude of someone who psychically has no determination, no direction. The attitude of Moses shows us the strength
inherent in abandonment. When Mary presents herself in the
temple in an attitude of full abandonment, she is indeed the
strong woman,[79] capable of burying herself in the mystery of
God's mercy. To bury oneself in the mystery of God's mercy is
to accept to disappear completely, to be buried in the sand so that
no trace be left. Moses buried the Egyptian in the sand precisely
so that nothing be seen, so that no trace be left. We must bury in
the sand our appetite for grandeur, power, domination, and fame.
As long as the "Egyptian" is not buried in the sand, we cannot
completely abandon ourselves. As long as the "Egyptian" is not
buried in the sand, we cannot arrive at the simplicity of sleep of
God's little child who surrenders completely to the Father's
mercy, knowing full well that is all that matters.

We know this speculatively, but practically there remains a
question: do we live as though the mercy of the Father is all that
matters? Do we not still lean upon our own strength, our own
virtues, upon a certain personal greatness and nobility? If we

79. Prv 31:10-31: "*mulierem fortem*"

still lean upon such things, let us ask Mary to give us the strength to kill the "Egyptian" and to bury him in the sand in order to live, with her, the attitude which Jesus asks of us in the Gospel. Jesus asks us to live like the flowers of the field in deep and complete abandonment, with no recourse to justice or human grandeur, with no desire to be noticed or understood.

Let us accept to be buried in the Father's mercy. This requires an heroic act. We do not immediately make it, but we must aim for it. Our Christian life is made for this. Such is the very spirit of religious vows, as of every Christian life. If religious vows do not enable us to reach full abandonment, then perhaps we live them "materially". Living the Christian life materially (that is, according to the letter), and living religious vows materially, without living their spirit, is always disastrous. As mother, Mary wishes to communicate to us this spirit. Such is her role as mother. She wishes to teach us the little way of true abandonment to the Father's mercy.

Abandonment: Evangelical Attitude of Spiritual Childhood

Mary's first act of cooperation with the Father's mercy is the act whereby she consecrates herself totally to God, body and soul, recognizing the absolute rights of divine mercy over her, recognizing the jealousy of divine mercy. This consecration takes place in abandonment. Abandonment is the "soul" of consecration which enables total surrender into the Father's hands. The mercy of God is recognized as primary and prevenient. Abandonment is rooted in an attitude of "littleness".

From a theological viewpoint we can see a progression in these three attitudes which, in reality, are one in Mary's soul. But in order to penetrate this mystery, we must consider the progression: consecration, abandonment, evangelical littleness. Evangelical littleness is to be understood as a mystery, that is, in its correspondence to the excessive love implied in mercy. Abandonment does not consist solely in receiving mercy.

Hidden in abandonment there must be an attitude of evangelical littleness which gives abandonment its ultimate note. Evangelical littleness consists in accepting precisely to be little, completely enveloped by the Father's love without seeing anything. Evangelical littleness consists in accepting not to see, to be borne only by mercy and love.

Such an attitude demands the cooperation of the three theological virtues: faith, which gives a sense of the rights of God's sovereign majesty and corresponds to consecration; hope, which is lived above all in abandonment, and love, which is expressed in littleness.

We see in the Gospel how greatly Jesus insists upon abandonment and littleness: "He who does not welcome the Kingdom of God as a little child will not enter."[80] Littleness is indeed, as it were, the foundation stone, the attitude which we must never lose or forget, an attitude which needs to be actualized as much as possible in order to enter the Kingdom of God. Littleness is not yet the mystery of silent, interior prayer, nor is it yet the Kingdom of God. It is the necessary condition to enter. To enter we must be totally surrendered to the Father's mercy in an attitude of littleness, an attitude of increasingly profound and loving littleness. God only shares His secrets with little ones.[81] God cannot share His secrets with others, with those who are not little. To enter the Kingdom of God is to enter His secrets.

The words of Jesus which state that he reveals His secrets to little ones show us that the mystery of Mary's consecration is above all, from Christ's perspective, a mystery of littleness and complete disappearance from before her own eyes, allowing the Father's mercy to embrace everything. This attitude of consecration in abandonment and littleness is truly that of a child. The servant must silence the "old man" to allow the Father's little child to abandon itself.

We have seen that the Old Testament shows us clearly the attitude of a servant. If the servant makes too much noise, the child

---

80. Mt 10:15; Lk 18:17
81. See Mt 11:25-26; Lk 10:21-22

cannot sleep. If the servant wants to take "adult " initiatives, initiatives of justice, if the servant wishes to use the Father's mercy as an "adult", with human greatness, he impedes the child from abandonment and littleness, and consequently impedes the Father's mercy from being exercised in plenitude.

Through Mary alone can abandonment and littleness — the fundamental attitude of the Christian life — be fully realized in us. We need to ask Mary to give us her motherly mercy, to envelop us. It is through her that the Father wants us to understand His mercy. Through the special maternal and enveloping mercy of Mary's heart, we experience in the most powerful and divine fashion the Father's mercy. It is therefore in consecrating ourselves and abandoning ourselves to Mary, in living evangelical littleness in her arms, that we will be completely abandoned in the arms of the Father. Mary is a mother who stoops to her little child and takes hold of it. Saint Louis De Montfort says that we must bury ourselves *in sinu Mariae*.[82] Such is evangelical littleness that can only be perfectly lived close to Mary and in her. She is given to us for this.

The Father willed that Mary fully experience evangelical littleness, thanks to the mystery of the Immaculate Conception. He willed that everything in her be marked by this littleness and that is why everything is so simple with her. There is always a battle in us if Mary is not present. If Mary leaves us, or more exactly, if we leave Mary, there will necessarily be a battle between the little child in us, who knows full well that it must abandon itself to the Father's mercy, and the "old man" who does not wish to be a servant, or is a poor servant, and claims to be a good servant and seeks to do great things based solely on justice. There will be a constant battle in us and we will not attain to the interior silence of littleness, we will not attain to full abandonment to the Father's mercy. We will not succeed in forgetting ourselves, as little children can do, living only the Father's mercy. By ourselves, we will not have the radical attitude that Jesus asks of us in a pressing, powerful fashion in the Gospel.

---

82. *True Devotion*, no. 18, 33, 156, 178, 199, 216, 243, 246, 248, 269. *The Secret of Mary* no. 14 & 54.

Mary alone can enable the "old man" in us to be silent, for only in her is the mystery of littleness fully realized, thanks to the Immaculate Conception. Mary is given to us by the Father so that, through her, we might attain to divine littleness and live by it. We are able to live this littleness only by means of her. Otherwise there will always be instability in us.

Littleness and abandonment require deep-seated stability, require being founded upon the rock. Persons who are truly abandoned, who live littleness, are stable. They remain stable through trial. God is their citadel[83]. There is continuity even if exterior circumstance changes completely. It is of little importance to them. The essential things remain for such persons and no one can touch them. There is an intimate secret between the Father and His little children. It is not even a secret. Little children cannot really bear secrets. There is something even more radical than a secret. There is, as it were, a deep attitude whereby the soul is borne by the Father's mercy.

Only Mary can give us this stability. When we think that we have acquired it by ourselves, apart from her, we are like Nicodemus and we ask, "How can I return to the womb?[84] It is impossible: I already know too many things. I am experienced and I have discovered many shortcomings in myself. It is impossible to be silent. The 'old man' is very rowdy and I have a vibrant personality. How am I to arrive at such littleness? How am I to be silent and not stare at myself? I can be very cumbersome for myself and for others. How then am I to attain to this full abandonment, to total consecration?" There is only one way and the Father shows it to us. The Father has given it to us. He makes of Mary His masterpiece of abandonment, of littleness, of consecration, so that it be only in her, and not by ourselves, that we too accomplish this act. We are incapable of consecrating ourselves. We are incapable of abandoning ourselves to God. The "old man" in us has desires and ambitions and aspirations that are very tenacious.

The secret, which, according to Saint Louis De Montfort[85] is truly a secret, is to plunge ourselves completely into Mary. The

83. Cf. Ps 46:59, 62, etc.
84. Cf. Jn 3:1 ff.
85. *The Secret of Mary*, no. 1

Father willed to show us His merciful omnipotence in and through the heart of Mary, so that it be through the heart of a mother that we understand it. Normally, a mother is prevenient for her child, that is, she plans and initiates. All motherly acts are acts which initiate. A mother initiates, envelops and bears her child. She is the one who bears any shocks or difficulties. She receives the blows. A child receives the impact through its mother when it is still in the mother's womb. This is the image which can perhaps help us to understand evangelical littleness.

Mary and Joseph: Radiance of Abandonment

Having consecrated and abandoned herself totally to God, and having surrendered herself to the Father's prevenient mercy, Mary communicates this very attitude to Joseph. How Joseph met Mary matters little here. Scripture tells us only one thing: Mary was "betrothed to Joseph"[86]. We know that this betrothal led to marriage and thus to a stable union, a stable unity. The betrothal is within Mary's consecration. Mary's consecration to God, the complete abandonment of her being, takes hold of Joseph's heart. It is indeed the first gift of fraternal charity that Mary gives. And it is very important to understand. This is what stabilizes a Christian community. A Christian community can only be stable in abandonment and littleness. If we reflect for a moment, we realize that any small or big division that occurs in fraternal charity always stems from a lack of abandonment. We were violent, for example. We sought to do justice to ourselves. We became proud and judgemental, asserting our own opinion and we introduced opposition. Abandonment fosters bonds and unity in fraternal charity.

The mystery of Mary's encounter with Joseph is the mystery of the dawn of the Christian community. It is, therefore, important to see where this community is situated and at what moment. It is just at the moment when Mary consecrates herself to God, abandons herself and lives this littleness. The Christian community is, as it were, a divine irradiation of it. Abandonment radiates. Anguish and anxiety also radiate, but in a totally different

---

86. Mt 1:18; Lk 1:27

fashion. When persons are agitated and anxious, around them is to be found a sort of whirlwind. All that is necessary is the agitation of one person for the entire milieu in which this person lives to become eventually agitated. Agitation engenders agitation, and very quickly takes hold of everything.

To this there is a remedy: abandonment. When there is in a family or in a community, a person who is truly abandoned, who lives intensely the mystery of abandonment, who lives it in a state of poverty like that of Mary's heart, the abandonment spreads, without this person even knowing it, for such a person is, as it were, a little child unaware of what he is doing. But the simple fact that this person lives this mystery of abandonment, creates silence around him. This is an observation like that which psychologists have made regarding children. The sleep of a child is the only thing that seems to be able to maintain silence in today's world. The world still respects the sleep of a child, at least in the family. We observe that a young woman who does not know what silence is learns it from her little child when she becomes a mother. This is a very beautiful and impressive psychological fact that we must transpose to the supernatural level. A person who is truly a child of Mary, who truly lives evangelical littleness, brings to the climate of a family, of a community, a certain demand for abandonment and divine silence, for total surrender into the hands of God. The demand for silence more or less gains territory, for there are always "Egyptians," that is, other persons who do not want such silence. The "old man" always makes a lot of noise. But if we are faithful, silence will be victorious.

This is what is shown to us in the Gospel in Mary's betrothal to Joseph. Spiritually speaking, Joseph steps into stride with Mary's rhythm. As regards the exterior, Joseph has a certain authority[87]. But in reality, Mary is the one who creates the atmosphere for their community and who gives it its true stability. Everything rests upon Mary. Joseph is relative to Mary. He is her guardian and her spouse. It is as Mary's spouse that the Holy Spirit first presents Joseph to us[88]. It is in being the spouse of the

---

87. See Mt 2:13, 14
88. Mt 1:19

heart of Mary that he can be her guardian. In order to be the guardian of the littleness and the abandonment of Mary, Joseph himself must necessarily enter into the same mystery of littleness and abandonment. We cannot be guardians of a mystery without living it ourselves, otherwise we will not be guardians, but, like the Egyptian[89], we will crush and suffocate it. As long as we have not penetrated this littleness and this abandonment, we will be tempted to say that they do not exist, that they are but dreams. We will prefer to defend human realities that can be seen, experienced, and which have results. Practically speaking, what we then do is adopt the approach of the "old man".

In order to be the guardian of Mary, the guardian of her consecration, her abandonment, and her littleness, it was necessary to live the same mystery. Through her abandonment to the Father's mercy, Mary draws Joseph's heart into the same life of abandonment. Joseph's heart is in unison with that of Mary. It was the first gift, the first act of Christian fraternal charity. The fraternal charity for Joseph, which flows from Mary's immaculate heart, is realized in this first gift.

In families we normally give gifts for different celebrations. For example, each time it is someone's birthday, the family members ask themselves what gift they might give. Divinely, the most beautiful gift that we can give is that of hiding ourselves in the heart of Mary like a little child who completely abandons itself in evangelical littleness, entirely surrendered to Mary. If we give this often, after a while the atmosphere of our community (or of our family) will be increasingly one which God desires, that is, one of littleness. This is very important, especially in our time. The Holy Spirit wishes to lead us more deeply into this attitude because the world, (not only the world, but alas, many priests and religious) no longer understand it. Often we extract from the Christian life nothing more than a sort of humanism. There is a certain return to the Old Testament and sometimes to the *mores* of the "Egyptians." We no longer seem to consider the Old Testament in relation to the New Testament. We consider the Old Testament in its psychological

89. Cf. Ex 2:11

richness and no longer understand the mystery and secret of the New Testament: evangelical littleness. We no longer understand the secret of abandonment which consists in totally surrendering through the heart of Mary, to the mercy of the Father.

This mystery of abandonment, of consecration in abandonment, and this mystery of fraternal charity reveal to us the twofold blossoming of charity in Mary's heart. Under the inspiration of the Holy Spirit, her heart is given as completely as possible to God, to the Father. She abandons her heart to His mercy, surrendering herself without restriction. Under the inspiration of the same Holy Spirit, Mary gives her heart to Joseph, giving to him the treasure of her heart, communicating to him her secret, that is, the work that God has wrought in her: her abandonment, her consecration. This gift to the Father comes about in the most divine and personal fashion. Mary presents herself to the Father, and her entire being is consecrated to Him. The gift to neighbor, the fruit of fraternal charity, is also realized in the most divine and personal fashion. Mary chooses Joseph and she accepts to be chosen by him without retracting the prior gift of herself to the Father. In fact, the more we are given to God, the more we are capable of being given to other persons. In order for the quality and the intensity of this fraternal charity to be perfect, it is translated into this preferential love of spouses in its purest and greatest aspect.

Saint Thomas Aquinas, in the footsteps of the Fathers of the Church, specifies that between Mary and Joseph there was a true marriage, "for the form of marriage consists in a certain indivisible conjunction between souls whereby each party is held to fidelity to the other in an indivisible manner.[90]" This union of souls existed perfectly between Mary and Joseph. Mary loved Joseph in order to love God even more. In loving Joseph, she did not retract anything from God. In fact, Joseph enabled her love for the Father to be even more hidden, more reserved, and more consecrated. Behold the wonderful covenant between these two loves in Mary's heart, the love of the evangelical law which unites these two loves in a single precept.

---

90. *ST* III q. 29, a. 2

Mary,

Mystery of Mercy

3

Annunciation

Annunciation

The mystery of the Annunciation reveals the third act of the Father's mercy for Mary: the gift that the Father gives, that is, His Son. It also reveals that only children can receive the Father's gift, that only children can receive the Father's secrets.[91] God is not content only to envelop us with prevenient mercy, with mercy that educates us. God wants us to cooperate so that we might penetrate to the very heart of His personal mystery, the Trinity, and live it. The Father's mercy is ordered to His love. It comes forth from His love and returns to it. His mercy is therefore necessary to penetrate the mystery of the Trinity.[92]

The Father's Mercy: The Gift of His Son

In order to show Nicodemus the essential character of the new law, Jesus reveals to him that God so loved the world that He gave His only begotten Son.[93] Let us consider how the Father gives His Son.

God first gives His Son to Mary, jealously, in secret. Here we once again find the great "law of mercy." He then gives His Son to all of humanity. The Father gives us His Son through Mary. According to divine wisdom, the Son must first be entirely entrusted to Mary whose mystery of abandonment, consecration, and littleness prepared and disposed her to receive the gift. In giving His Son, the Father gives Himself. He can only give Himself in this way. The gift of His Son expresses the excessive love in His heart as Father. In order to give oneself, one must love with perfect, complete love. Only love which reaches perfection allows for a personal gift, the gift of self. The Father gives Himself with complete love. He gives Himself to humanity as Father, and in order to give Himself as Father, He must give

---

91. See Mt 11: 25-26; Lk 10:21-22
92. We will not enter the debate about current exegetical interpretations of the angel's words to Mary. The interpretation of the fathers of the Church and, in their footsteps, Thomas Aquinas, (*ST* III, q. 30, a. 1) seems to express well the living thought of the Church.
93. Jn 3:16

Himself in and through His Son. Through the Son we receive the Father. We cannot receive the Father independently of the Son.[94]

In revealing the mystery of the Father, the Annunciation reveals the mystery of the Trinity and thereby leads to the source of the contemplative life. The contemplative life is inseparable from the Father's gift of His Son and from the revelation of the mystery of the Trinity. We are sometimes tempted to oppose contemplation of Christ and contemplation of the Trinity. Such oppositions are superficial, for every act of truly supernatural contemplation necessarily introduces the one who contemplates into the mystery of the Trinity. Indeed, there can be no act of contemplation without the gift of the Father being received — whether or not it be accompanied by an experience of each Divine Person.

In giving His Son, the Father gives Himself totally. Not only does He perform an act of infinitely great and wonderful prevenient mercy, but He gives Himself substantially. God alone is substantial love and substantial gift in His entire being. In Him alone the gift is perfect. Outside of Him every gift remains very limited. A creature cannot give itself totally, for it is not only love. A fundamental self-centeredness paralyzes the creature in its most generous "élans." Indeed, a gift achieves love in its most perfect aspect. We can try to examine love at the metaphysical level, but we only truly understand it in living it. We only truly grasp it in a personal experience. In order to comprehend better, the human intellect always divides what is simple. Love is simple. Is not the simplicity of God ultimately the simplicity of His goodness and His love? When we leave divine love, we complicate everything. Once we return to divine love we simplify everything by unifying it.

In reality love is simple. We must not separate the elements which stem from philosophical analysis. Starting from our experience of spiritual, human love we discern two primary aspects. Love first implies full receptivity of the person loved. Love renders us welcoming. Indeed, we can only be truly welcoming to the extent we love. Someone who does

94. Jn 14:23; 14:21; 8:15; 10:23; 14:7-11; Mt. 11:27; Lk 10:22

not love becomes incapable of welcoming others, of truly receiving others. Someone who does not love turns in on himself, withdraws, becomes entangled in his own self-centeredness, and thus becomes a stranger to others. Self-centeredness hardens us by enclosing us in our own limits. True love orders us to the one we love by "connaturalizing" us to him. Boundaries disappear, and a certain oneness comes about. Hence, as love renders us welcoming, it also has us come out of ourselves. It has us tend and move towards the one we love. Such is the second aspect of love: ecstasy.[95] At first glance, this coming out of self seems to be opposed to welcoming. Normally we must "stay at home", we must remain within ourselves in order to welcome. And yet these two movements are one. To go before the friend is the best way to receive him. To do so is to anticipate the welcome. A complete welcome only exists with love which includes this coming out of self. Otherwise, we welcome the person in a possessive fashion and consequently do not really welcome; we do not respect the other person in his otherness. Love is a substantial gift and when perfect, and includes these two aspects. That is why, according to Saint Thomas Aquinas, love can only be fully realized in friendship. Friendship exists when a person loves not only someone loveable, but someone who loves in return. The love is then not only for someone capable of attracting, but for someone actually living this mutual love.

It is only in the Trinity that love is realized in its perfection. The Father gives Himself completely to His Son, in the Son's eternal generation. He gives Him all that He has and, at the same time, He is "welcome" for His Son, truly substantial welcome. Indeed, the Son never leaves the Father. The Son is *apud Patrem*, that is, He dwells, He lives forever close beside the Father. Being welcome, the Father gives Himself completely to His Son in an ecstasy of love. All that the Father possesses belongs to the Son. Reciprocally, the Son Himself is welcome and gift for the Father. Having received everything from the

---

95. *ST* 1; I- II, q. 28 a. 3, II-II q. 175, a. 2, ad, 1

Father, He is entirely given to the Father. In this magnificent and extraordinary "cycle" of the Trinity, we can say that the Son is in the Father and the Father is in the Son.[96] When we give ourselves, we have the impression that the person who receives our gift only receives. However, in perfect love, the one who receives, in return, gives everything, and the one who gives himself becomes welcome for the one who receives. The Son is all-welcome for the Father, substantial welcome, such that, as the Son lives close beside the Father, so the Father lives close beside the Son, in the Son, in the Word, in the *Logos*. The Holy Spirit is this mutual welcome, this mutual gift. The Holy Spirit is the substantial and personal Welcome of the Father and the Son. The Holy Spirit is Ecstasy, reciprocal Gift, the Fruit of their mutual welcome, of their mutual ecstasy. The Holy Spirit is ultimate oneness.[97]

In the mystery of the Annunciation the Father gives His Son to Mary. And in order that this mystery extend into her heart, Mary, under the inspiration of the Holy Spirit, gives herself entirely in an act of loving ecstasy. She forgets herself in order to be close beside the Word, and so that the Word be close beside her. In receiving the One who is the Gift of the Father, she herself becomes gift and welcome. Saint Thomas Aquinas says that the mystery of the Annunciation involves a mission,[98] the temporal mission to which the Father destines His Son. In the mission, the eternal procession of the Son terminates in the heart of Mary, the heart of a creature. The same gift, eternally realized in the Trinity, the gift that the Father gives to the Son, is prolonged in the heart of Mary. However, the gift takes on a particular form: that of mercy, for it terminates in a creature, which it transforms.

Indeed, the Father cannot give His Son to a creature without the gift being an act of mercy. There can only be pure gift in the Trinity. Outside of the Trinity, the Father's gift of His Son is necessarily accompanied by mercy, unique and wonderful

---

96. Jn 14:10
97. See *ST* I q. 37, a. 1; q. 38 a. 1 and 2
98. *ST* I q. 43, a. 2

mercy. The Father can give no greater or more absolute gift: giving His Son to a creature and giving Him as Son, as He Himself, the Father, possesses Him eternally. The mercy which envelops the Father's gift at the Annunciation is realized and manifested precisely in the wonderful "adaptation" of the Incarnation. The Father wishes to give His Son to Mary in such a way that she receive Him as perfectly as possible. In her, the Word assumes human nature, the Word becomes flesh. In order for the gift to be perfect, Mary is called to cooperate with it in her own way. The Father's supreme mercy — which is infinitely delicate and tender — requires that the person who receives, cooperate in this work of mercy so that it might become his or her own, all the while remaining something to which he or she has no right. Such a gift is received gratuitously. It is a gift which is also the most intimate fruit of the person's labor. Jesus is the Son of God. He is the gift of the Father. If the Father gives His Son to a creature and calls the creature to cooperate fully with the gift, the creature must be able to look at the Son as does the Father, that is, as his or her only son. Now, a creature can only look at the Word, the eternal Son of the Father, as her own son by becoming mother of His body, mother of the human nature that He assumes, and mother of the Word who assumes human nature.

Divine Motherhood: Source of Contemplative Life

In the light of this Fatherly mercy, the mystery of Mary's motherhood emerges as a reflection, as a living image of the eternal fatherhood of God with regard to the Word. Mary indeed receives in an adequate and deep, tender and merciful fashion the gift that the Father gives to her of His Son out of pure gratutiousness. If, in His wisdom, the Father wishes to perform an act of absolute mercy, an act which, in a certain sense, exhausts the demands of mercy, it is "necessary" that Mary become mother of the Incarnate Word. This motherhood is truly the most efficacious and intimate cooperation of a creature with

God. In the realm of human realities, there is no deeper or more fundamental connaturality, there is no greater adaptation than that between child and mother. According to the "laws" of motherhood, as God willed them, a child is part of its mother. All the while possessing its own being, all the while being another person with its own autonomy, its own spiritual and individualized soul, a child remains nevertheless "something of its mother". Even after birth, as it grows, a child is radically and fundamentally dependent on its mother. There remains a mysterious bond precisely because of this radical, reciprocal adaptation. A child prolongs the life of its mother. A child is, as it were, the irradiation of its mother's life; and this vital conjunction which existed in the beginning, in a certain way, continues.

In His mercy, God uses motherhood to make of a creature the mother of God. Can we go so far as to say that God willed motherhood for this? Why did God ultimately will that the human species propagate as it does in this way? Why did God establish this mysterious bond between child and mother? Why did He make the hearts of mothers so merciful towards their children? Why is a child initially buried in the womb of its mother? Is it not ultimately in order that a creature, in unique, personal intimacy, might cooperate with the Father's gift of His Son? When the Father gave His Son there needed to be a mother to receive and live by Him as a mother receives and lives by her child. In the light of divine wisdom, we can say that motherhood was perhaps willed by God with a view to Mary's motherhood, a unique and divine motherhood, more perfect than all others, a motherhood which measures all others. In the light of divine wisdom, all other instances of motherhood find their full meaning in this motherhood. It would be insufficient to say that God makes use of motherhood as of a purely extrinsic means. In reality, He willed human motherhood with a view to this ultimate and perfect motherhood. How wonderfully then this act of extraordinary mercy enables us to understand the greatness of the Christian family.

Indeed, if God had not created motherhood, the Incarnation

would not have come about in this fashion. God could have created a human species that multiplies differently — not an impossibility. It is impossible, however, that an angel become mother of God, that an angel experience the intimacy that Mary experienced with God. God, therefore, left man, even after original sin, the possibility of cooperating with His creative action. Such is the meaning of Eve's words after the birth of her first son, "I have produced a man with the help of the Lord."[99] With all human motherhood there is cooperation with the almighty work of Creation, for God creates the soul in the future human body, rooted deeply in the womb. God thus disposed all things so that a creature might be the living image of His fatherhood in the Trinity. In becoming mother, Mary must welcome the Father's Son as the Father welcomes Him eternally. Mary's entire being must become a "welcome" of the Father's gift. She must give herself entirely and, in this very gift, offer all her strength. Everything in her must be "ecstasy" in order to receive this gift, the Fruit of the Father's eternal ecstasy. She must be surrendered to the gift which establishes her as mother of the Father's Son.

In the "fiat" of the Annunciation — a "fiat" of living faith, of loving faith in the Father's gift — begins Christian contemplative life, a life directly nourished by this substantial gift. God willed that this life be given in this way. The Father's contemplation is fatherly: the Father, as Father, contemplates the Son and the Son, as Son, contemplates the Father. The mystery of the Trinity is a contemplative, familial mystery of welcome and personal gift. God introduces His creature into His fatherly contemplation, into His familial mystery. Thus, we can understand how the contemplation of His creature can be motherly. In the "fiat" at the Annunciation, Mary's contemplation is motherly. This is true, in a certain sense, of all Christian contemplation. All Christian contemplation possesses something of this motherly mode. The Father gives us Mary's contemplative life as a model in order to show us the full realization of Christian contempla-

---

99. Gn 4:1

tion here on earth. Plenary contemplation will only be possible in heaven in the beatific vision where contemplation, nevertheless, keeps this motherly mode. Mary remains mother even in her beatific contemplation. To assert that contemplation is an act of intellect and consequently that Mary's contemplation is only in the summit of her intellect, and that her motherhood is secondary, is to confuse Christian contemplation with philosophical contemplation. Christian contemplation is founded on faith and blossoms in the gift of wisdom, which is a loving knowledge of the mystery of God. Now, Mary's motherhood is not extrinsic to her faith. Her motherhood terminates in the Incarnate Word and, therefore, in God. In faith, Mary cooperates with a gift from divine fatherhood, that is, she receives the Father's gift in faith[100] and conceives it in her heart, as St. Augustine says. Her faith is, therefore, motherly, for it is a cooperation with God's fatherhood regarding the Word become flesh, a cooperation which is, above all, a welcoming of the word of God as the word of God, with tremendous purity.

Divine Motherhood: Act of Contemplative Faith

We must often come back to the purity of Mary's faith in order to grasp the essence of contemplative faith in its two aspects: child and mother. Mary receives the gift of the Father in faith through the words of an angel. She leans upon these words. Any and every adherence in faith leans, or rests, upon divine words, given so that we might attain to the reality beyond them, to the *res divina*.[101] Without ever bypassing revelation (the Scriptures), we nevertheless need to go beyond its material expression in order to reach, through it, the reality of the mystery. Such is Mary's attitude at the Annunciation. In response to the words of the angel, she said *fiat mihi secundum verbum tuum*, "Be it done unto me according to thy word." This *fiat* expresses her act of faith. Mary adheres divinely to the words of the angel, that is, to the very word of God. The angel is an emissary of God who is

---

100. *ST* III q. 30, a. 1
101. *ST* I q. 1, a. 3, ad 1; II-II q. 1, a. 1; q. 2, a. 2

not in competition with God. Mary's wholly divine adherence is in direct reference to God. The words of the angel are the means, the sign willed by God to allow Mary to adhere to the Father's gift of Himself, which is the substantial, subsistent Word.

Mary's act of faith is the model of every act of contemplative faith, of every act of faith fully realized thanks to love and to the gifts of the Holy Spirit. Often our acts of faith do not have this quality or penetration because of a lack of attentiveness or generosity. Our acts of faith often remain a purely exterior adherence. We are content with reciting the Creed over and over. But such repetition does not deeply engage our life. Our acts of faith often remain imperfect because we think too much, due to a lack of love for the one speaking to us. Indeed, we adhere to the word of God, but without penetrating its intimate and deep meaning. Practically speaking, we believe, while measuring our adherence by our understanding of the word of God, by the understanding we have of the propositions of faith. Our act of faith does tend toward the mystery, but the consciousness of the act of faith is what interests us above all. Such overly rational, psychological self-reflection risks diminishing the realism and the absoluteness of the adherence of faith. Our acts of faith are imperfect and can remain so because we are not sufficiently surrendered to the love of God. We still "grope" in the darkness like beginners, concerned, above all, with exercising our faith in order to increase and intensify it. We do adhere to the word of God, with a desire to grasp its meaning, trying to understand and assimilate Jesus' teaching, meditating upon the Scriptures and comparing the various texts. This is good and necessary, but it is not yet contemplative faith.

Contemplative faith is loving faith which adheres to the very mystery of God out of love for the mystery itself. Contemplative faith adheres to the mystery of God by "receiving it", as John powerfully expresses it.[102] Loving faith receives the word of God, receives light, receives the gift of God, as Mary welcomed the Word of God in her "fiat." To receive the word of God as a liv-

---

102. Jn 1: 9-12

ing word is to receive the word as a divine seed, as the only light. It is to receive as did Mary, maternally, and to let it take hold of our intellect, to let it transfigure and enable our intellect to bear fruit. Between faith which reflects by reasoning and faith which receives by contemplating, we see the difference between the faith of a servant and the faith of a child and spouse. Contemplative faith jealously clings to this only light. It sets aside all others so that the intellect be illuminated by the light of God alone. If we stubbornly seek to possess other lights, the pure light of God can no longer be communicated as freely. If we cling to a particular way of praying, we will remain good and faithful servants, but we will never become little children who welcome the substantial light of the Father and contemplate it with love.

Mary's faith at the Annunciation was indeed the faith of a little child who welcomed the substantial light of the Father in order to live by it. Her act of faith is made in perfect purity. The Gospel clearly indicates this in setting in parallel the annunciation to Zechariah and his response and the annunciation to Mary and her response. The contrast is one that the fathers of the Church liked to underscore.[103]

Zechariah demands a sign. He forgot that the word of God in itself is a sign which leads to the mystery. We often proceed like Zechariah. We receive the word of God in a material or literal fashion and thus have need for another sign. We forget that the word of God is already an efficacious sign which leads us to the mystery. Zechariah seemed to be an excellent servant, a God-fearing man. He represents the Old Testament and, at the same time, brings it to completion, for he becomes the father of John the Baptist, the precursor. We can see in Zechariah those who wish to hold faithfully and exclusively to the light of the Old Testament. This is very enlightening, and helps us not to reduce the demands of the New Testament to those of the Old Testament, which "psycholigism" and certain "scientific" interpretations do too easily. The Old Testament formed servants

---

103. Lk 1:5-22, 26-38

who had not arrived at spiritual childhood. These faithful servants had not arrived at living the mystery of evangelical littleness which enables to receive the word of God as the divine sign which leads to the Father's gift of His Son. They remained in the messianic realm, a temporal messianism. They thought that God would send a great prophet to accomplish great things, to deliver the people of Israel in a temporal fashion. They awaited entrance into a land of superabundance, where milk and honey flow, believing a promise that they had understood in a material fashion.[104]

A servant is indeed a man of faith and hope, but his faith is exercised in a human way, leaning upon arguments of human reason, demanding absolutely sure arguments, for, in him, prudence presides. Moreover, when he finds himself before words which seem incoherent at first, he demands signs. He wants to be absolutely sure. Zechariah seeks by his own virtue to be absolutely sure. But God demands more. He awaits faith that is more trusting and more abandoned. God awaits, as it were, a surpassing of excessively prudential reflection. It can happen that excessive prudence become the enemy of true, supernatural prudence which is exercised under the motion of the gift of counsel. Moral virtue must normally be a disposition to the contemplative life. Sought for itself, moral virtue can become an obstacle. This is what we see with Zechariah. He subsequently becomes incapable of immediately receiving the words of the angel as the word of God, as the will of God for him. He does not understand and thus asks for a sign. And as God loves Zechariah, His faithful and prudent servant, He corrects him. He has him enter the contemplative life via a purgative path, in a "negative" fashion. He renders him mute… mute as regards human prudence. Zechariah wanted to show himself prudent, but God wanted to show him divine prudence. He renders Zechariah mute so that he understand that he must silence his personal judgement before the demands of God's love, of God's word. God has Zechariah pass through the "narrow door" of mutism. God gives him a sign, a

104. Ex 3:8; Lv 20:24

penal sign.[105] The servant who lacks littleness and abandonment always risks not understanding that what God wills can surpass human reason and human prudence, even enlightened by faith. Such a servant always seeks certitude in continuity with the certitudes of reason. He asks for signs. He understands with difficulty the absoluteness of the adherence of faith. Faith in itself is a certitude, but a certitude which accepts that which is without evidence, without obviousness, in order to be buried in God. It is a loving certitude in divine mercy alone.[106]

Mary is a child of God, totally abandoned, little, totally surrendered to mercy, and thus does not need a sign. She can accept directly the words of the angel without reasoning or discussing. These words are the very measure of her adherence of faith. Mary does not reason about faith. She does not measure her adherence by what she knows. She did not say, "I accept to become the mother of God according to my understanding." Mary accepts "blindly" the word of God as a little child, entirely receptive. In order to carry the word of the Father as a mother carries her child, she receives the word in faith. She opens her intellect divinely to the mystery of the gift of the Word. She welcomes the Word of God, the Son of the Father as the only light for her intellect, as its very source, more intimate than intellect is to itself. She opens her intellect to the light of the Word by accepting momentarily to see nothing. The light of God is given in the darkness of faith and Mary accepts that her intellect become entirely receptive, in fact, pure receptivity, a pure receptacle of the Word of God.

Thomas Aquinas specifies that an act of faith is an adherence to the word of God.[107] This act of faith occurs in receptivity. It consists in receiving the word of God as good soil receives the seed. Jesus himself used this comparison[108] to express the maternal aspect of faith. Earth is maternal. We indeed speak of Mother Earth. She receives the seed. The word of God is given as a seed which demands to take possession of our intellect, in its most fundamental aspect. The intellect is normally what is most autonomous in us. It is the root of all autonomy and of every right

105. *ST* II-II q. 97, a. 2, ad. 3
106. Heb. 11:1
107. *ST* II-II q. 2, a. 1.
108. Mt 13:23, Lk 8:15, Mk 4:20

of possession. In judging we posses. From a human viewpoint, the right to possess is a consequence of our capacity to judge. All possession occurs in judgement (or discernment). The intellect has a fundamental "law": that of this vital assimilation which has the intellect grasp and draw to itself all that it knows. That is why the intellect is the principle of all vital autonomy in us. Through faith, Mary's intellect accepts entirely different *mores*, those of "good soil." Mary accepts not to "understand" and to become pure receptivity with respect to the One who is the source, the principle of her intellect: the Word. Mary accepts completely this dependence, to receive all determination from God, to have no determination of her own, no judgement of her own. Indeed, in the mystery of the Annunciation, Mary's intellect has no other determination than that of the Word, and this occurs in absolute purity. Her intellect has no other physiognomy, no other "face" than that of the Word. Mary adheres directly to the Word in using the words of the angel as an instrument. These words become her support, but a support which is immediately surpassed. These words enable her to adhere fully to the Word who gives Himself to her in absolute silence, the silence of a little child conceived in its mother. It is in order to awaken in Mary's intellect this wonderfully maternal attitude that the Word of God gives Himself in this way. Mary's intellect is captivated by the Word of God. Mary lets herself be entirely relative to the Word, having no other orientation than the Word Himself.

The words of a messenger of God must be received with love as a sign, as a sign capable of uniting us intimately to the mystery of God Himself. In her act of faith at the Annunciation, Mary gives us a model of the clear and simple faith of a little child whose intellect is "silent" in order to be entirely receptive and attentive to the gift of the Father. She experiences no agitation, no human "cogitatio," no thoughts, no human judgement which would impede her soul from becoming the "good soil" where the Father wishes to sow the Word, His Son, the divine Seed given in plenitude to Mary.

The second characteristic of Mary's faith is its extreme realism. The Father reveals His mystery to Mary by drawing her into it. God never gives us a revelation so that it might remain foreign to us. When God reveals a mystery to us, He introduces us into it. He has us understand that the mystery is given. He connaturalizes us to it. The great revelation of the Trinity, the revelation of the mystery of God in its most personal aspect is given here in a wonderfully fatherly teaching. God introduces His little girl into His inmost mystery by asking of her the service of motherhood. He asks her to receive in faith His beloved Son so that the Son might be her beloved son as well. The Word given to Mary takes hold of her human person like a child takes hold of its mother. The word of God is communicated by incarnating itself in her, by taking possession of her.

The Father can only reveal Himself through the Son and the Son can only reveal His Father. Both are mutually relative in the Trinity. For the first time, the Father reveals Himself as personally distinct from the Son. In so doing, He reveals who the Son is. Now, He reveals His Son in order to give Him to Mary as son. And he reveals Himself as Father in order to draw Mary into the inmost mystery of His fatherly fruitfulness by making of her the mother of His only Son. Here we touch upon the extraordinary realism of faith. Faith is not abstract knowledge. Faith always implies a commitment. We cannot consider the mysteries of faith as pure spectators, as we would mathematical truths, for example. When we know a truth in a purely intelligible and abstract fashion, we possess its richness in a purely intentional fashion. The realism of the adherence of faith is much deeper, for faith is a participation in the knowledge of God, in His light, in the mystery of His contemplation. And the contemplation of God is not of the intentional realm, but of the divine realm. It is reality in its most powerful and most loving aspect. The contemplation of God is the mystery of God Himself, mystery of light and of love.

As a participation in the contemplation of God, the knowledge of faith engenders in us the divine desire to live the very life of God. Faith has us grasp that our life cannot only be a human life, cannot only have philosophical knowledge, as pure and elevated as it might be, but that it must imply a union, an intimate conjunction with the very mystery of the Father. In this sense we can say the knowledge of faith tends towards connaturalizing us to the mystery of the Father, to the mystery of contemplation of the triune God, for it is in contemplating that the Father engenders His Son and gives Himself to Him. It is here that the knowledge of faith is akin to love. Faith seeks to occur in contemplation, in a personal gift of love. It is not because the knowledge of faith remains enveloped in darkness that we must conclude that it is abstract knowledge. We often see what is abstract very clearly. Faith has us adhere to the mystery in obscurity, demanding the sacrifice of all obviousness. We must accept to be, as it were, blind, or better yet, like little children who have not yet seen the face of their father, but who know that he is present, that he is given to them, that he opens to them the treasures of his infinitely merciful heart, of his life as father. The Father is infinitely present not only as Creator. In His immanence as Creator, He communicates intimately, from within, His Son, His light and His love.

At the Annunciation, Mary manifests the realism of faith. Her act of faith engages her completely in the mystery of the Father. The deep orientation of her life changes with this revelation. Until then, her life was expectation and abandonment. Now divine contemplation takes hold of her life. Indeed, contemplation does not eliminate abandonment, but it demands a greater attitude of faith and hope which leans immediately upon the mercy of the Father who gives His Son, who gives His light.

The Word, substantial Light, who was incarnated in Mary, continues to take hold of us, to take possession of us as His living members so that we may be one with Him. The great mystery of the Incarnation extends into us, in and through faith. Through faith, we become living members of Christ. We participate intimately in His life. With Him we form "one mystical Person"[109]. Complete commitment of our life implied in faith

---

109. *ST* III, q. 19, a. 4, q. 48, a. 2, ad. 1, q. 49, a. 2; *De Veritate* q. 29, a. 7, ad. 11; Commentary on the Epistle to the Ephesians 1, 24 (no. 61)

ends in a union comparable to that of vine and branches. This deep union must normally and progressively change the life of our heart into that of Christ's heart, the life of our intellect into that of Christ's intellect. All the light that the Father gives to His Son becomes our light. All the love that the Father gives to the Son becomes our love.

Nevertheless, we do not see [with clarity]. And not seeing the greatness of the mystery, we always risk living in a lesser way the realism of faith, living an abstract "human" faith. The strategy of the Devil is that of reducing us to faith that is insufficiently divine, of having us pass from the faith of a child to that of a servant, and thereby to a purely human faith. The Devil proceeds in this fashion because he only has natural faith, intellectual faith capable of observing the evidence of signs, but not faith which adheres lovingly to the mystery. His acquired faith, or better, his "angelic" faith, angelic in the sense that Satan still has the intellect of an angel, is a terribly "natural" faith. Forced and constrained by the evidence of signs, he asserts the existence of facts, of occurrences, because he cannot do otherwise without denying his own intellect. But he does not penetrate the mystery. His faith is not supernatural. He is obliged to recognize that God has given His Son to humanity, that God was incarnated in Mary and continues to take hold of us as His own members. He is obliged to recognize the existence of the Mystical Body, but this mystery does not touch him. It remains distant[110]. Mercy is intolerable for him. His strategy, therefore, consists in drawing us into faith similar to his abstract intellectual faith. With such faith man recognizes that there exist signs of credibility. He knows that it is "possible," that it would be nice if it were this way. If he is intelligent, he knows that Christianity appears to be the most "perfect" religion. To such a person the Gospel seems quite beautiful and very harmonious, but it remains, nevertheless, exterior and distant, if he stops only at motives for credibility[111].

The Devil always attempts, in one way or another, to ravage

---

110. *ST* I, q.64, a. 2, ad. 5, II-II, q. 5, a. 2, q. 18, a. 3, ad. 2, III q. 76, a. 7
111. *ST* I, q. 3, a. 1, ad. 1, II-II, q. 6, a. 1

the absolute simplicity of our faith, our faith as children, pure and realistic faith, which understands that God is the only reality and that the Father's gift demands of us the total commitment of our life. The Devil primarily tries to have us pass from this simple faith to faith which demands judgement and reasoning and signs. Then, little by little, he tries to lead us to lose our faith. This is how he ruins faith in today's world. His strategy is always the same. It is rather comprehensible from a theological viewpoint. As is said in theology, we can only act according to what we are: *agens agit simile sibi*. When the Devil tempts, he can only act in this way. No longer having divine faith, he cannot know what faith is. He does know, however, what natural faith is. He thus tries, in every way possible, to draw us out of the contemplative attitude of faith, to lower us progressively to "reasonable", prudential faith. From there it is easy for him to lead us to reject the last remnants of faith.

It is important for us to understand that as long as faith remains subordinated, in its exercise, to a human mode, (such as the faith of Zechariah) that is, too dependent upon human reason, upon human prudence, it is necessarily exercised in an imperfect fashion. As long as our faith remains dependent, in its adherence, upon signs, as long as we do not go beyond signs, to adhere to the word of God as word of God, to adhere to the revealed mystery, our faith remains imperfect and consequently does not totally engage our lives. From here comes a division between faith and love. However, contemplative faith, faith realized under the motion of the Holy Spirit by the gift of knowledge, is loving faith, faith which engages our whole life, which takes hold of us. Such faith is truly that of little children[112].

Contemplative Faith of Mary:
Source of Silence

The extraordinarily pure and realistic faith, which engages Mary's whole life, draws her intellect into total silence. Silence is the property, the contemplative quality, the fruit of faith.

---

112. See Lk 18:17, Mk 10:15, Mt 19:14

When she receives the word of God, Mary must be silent. She must be silent even with respect to Joseph to whom her mystery of abandonment binds her so deeply and who was given to her to be her guardian. The mystery of faith binds Mary to the Father in such a way that she must be silent vis-à-vis Joseph. Mary is plunged into the substantial silence of the Trinity. The Father communicates His Son in silence, without vain words, drawing into this very silence.

It is important to understand this silence, the silence of children (children, once again, in the evangelical sense). As there is the abandonment of children, there is also, it seems, the contemplation of children, contemplation which is realized and which blossoms in interior, divine silence which is the immediate consequence of the intensity and purity of contemplative faith. It is only in silence that loving faith can be fully exercised, fully lived. The gift of the Father, his substantial Secret, can only be communicated to such silent faith.

Now the only way to enter positively into silence is to keep a secret, to bear a secret. Noise is the consequence of movement. All vital movement is normally exercised according to a certain rhythm. Consequently, as regards our sensitivity, as regards the sensitive dimension of our human person, exterior silence necessarily entails privation. It is said of children that they are very "lively" when they move a lot, when they make a lot of noise. We often resemble children in this way. We like to manifest that we are alive by making noise. We do so in all sorts of activities, even activities of the intellect. We like to tell ourselves stories, to carry on an interior "dialogue". If we are not careful, we begin to do this spontaneously, creating for ourselves an interior companion, to prove to ourselves that we are "alive." The human being, a rational animal, does not like exterior silence. Exterior silence imposes itself as a privation and easily becomes for him a presentiment of death and emptiness. Our human nature hates death and emptiness. One need but look around to observe how those who live primarily at the level of sensation fear silence. Today's world, which has lost, for the most part, the interior life, is increasingly afraid of silence. Even for contemplatives, exterior silence would be unbearable if it were not the sign and the demand of something deeper, that is, interiorization. Interior, mystical silence is not rest without an act of faith, for it is a silence which stems from the intensity of loving faith. It is, as it were, the interior result of a heart that loves intensely. It is, as it were, the fruit, the normal "expression" of an intellect which has received the secret of the Father. The presence in our hearts of a secret to be kept brings about this special dimension, this density which is interior silence.

This is already true at the human level. It is an experience that you may have had. You may perhaps recall the first secret entrusted to you. As a child, someone shared something important with you and added, "Above all, keep the secret!" and at that moment you felt as though you were "someone". You were told that you alone knew, and thus understood that you were truly "someone," someone who was trusted, someone capable of receiving a secret and keeping it. This particular something separated you from others and bound you to the person who entrusted the secret. This is the deep law of secrets from a psychological viewpoint. A secret binds us to the person who entrusts it to us and, at the same time, separates us from other persons. A secret brings about this separation and this unity. A secret engenders silence of a unique quality. For, although we can speak to the person who entrusted the secret to us, we must, to the extent we are to keep the secret, remain silent *vis-á-vis* other persons. That is why secrets are sometimes hard to bear.

In the human realm, secrets are always the fruit of affective knowledge. They exist only in the "practical" realm. They are always contingent truths. This accounts for their seductive quality. There are no secrets in mathematics or in philosophy. Secrets are, in a certain sense, the gem of our hearts, the fragile fruit, which cannot be separated from its living source without killing it (and which dies when separated from the source), for we only communicate secrets to a friend, to someone who is one with our own heart. Communication of secrets is the sign of friendship[113], the sign which manifests and proves the friendship and the total trust of a friend. Moreover, in the human realm, secrets are limited. We may have had the impression at times that the whole universe would collapse if we were to betray a secret entrusted to us. This impression stems from the fact that it is proper to affective knowledge to capture our vitality. In fact, a secret remains something very contingent and it remains possible to escape it, so to speak, and seek refuge in the realm of art or speculative knowledge. Such escape or evasion may be necessary for the person who bears heavy secrets in order to maintain a certain balance. Finally, it is important to note, especially as we try to apply this analogically to our situations as Christians in the Church, the important meaning of secrets during times of war. In such times secrets bind a network of defenders of the same cause and separate them from other persons, especially enemies. Betrayal precisely consists in surrendering the secret to the enemy and thus introducing the enemy into the network. It is thus that Eve, by communicating to the Serpent the precept of God, which was the secret of this first "human society" between her and Adam, truly betrays and introduces the Devil into their intimacy. From a human psychological viewpoint, secrets are always linked to love and are inseparable from love. Without love there is no secret. A secret is truly the common fruit of knowledge and love, binding us to the one who communicates it, and separating us from others.

Let us transpose these remarks to the supernatural level. The knowledge of faith is an affective knowledge. For the heart of a child who welcomes the Father whom he knows loves him, every divine word becomes a secret which binds him to the Father. This is what we see in the Annunciation. The Father intimately draws Mary into His mystery by communicating His secret, His Son, the personal secret of His life as Father. Herein lies the difference with human secrets. Secrets can only be

---

113. *Contra Gentiles*, IV ch. 21; Commentary on the Gospel of John 15, no. 2016

"substantial" as we say, in the supernatural order. Such secrets both regard what is most intimate and profound in our intellect and dictate the practical attitude we are to have in our daily lives. Mary receives the words which God communicates through the angel, the gift that the Father gives, as a substantial secret which binds her to God, which divinely encloses her in the mystery of the Father. Such is the "reclusion" of faith. Every truly contemplative act of faith encloses us in God, in His mystery and fashions in us, as it were, a divine rampart, separating us from all that is not the mystery of the Father.

The Son, the secret *par excellence* of God, can only be communicated by God as a secret and demands to be received as such. Mary's faith life is marked by this secret which hides her in the eyes of all, her own and those of others, for it escapes the jurisdiction of human intellect, of critical judgement. Before this divine secret, the intellect is silent. That is why only children can receive it. "Adults," the "wise and learned," those who are too intelligent in their own eyes, cannot receive the secret without seeking to analyze it. Curiosity of wisdom and human prudence incite such persons to explore and, as it is not appropriate to throw "pearls to swine,"[114] the Father cannot communicate His secret to such prudence which seeks to posses the secret. God cannot share divine secrets with a human intellect that does not accept to be completely silent in order to receive them only in a maternal faith. With respect to divine secrets, one must always be somewhat maternal. When we truly love something, do we not jealously hide it? Entrusting His secret to Mary, the Father asks that she jealously keep it, as a mother. That is why Mary is silent even with respect to Joseph. Indeed she continues to love him and her affection is in no way diminished. In abandonment she remains for him exactly what she was before. In receiving the secret of the Father, she is even more abandoned, for her abandonment acquires in her act of contemplation a note of greater intensity. But, Mary is silent. She is alone to live this divine secret without posing questions,

---

114. Mt 7:6

without asking if others have been forewarned. Such curiosity would hinder her from jealously keeping the secret of God as it demands to be kept.

We must try to penetrate the silence of Mary at the Annunciation. With this divine secret, the contemplative life begins. It is the first full secret that God communicates. Until then the secrets were partial and did not have the same demand. That is why the contemplative life had not yet blossomed in believers, who were above all servants. It is with the gift of the Son that the contemplative life blossoms. It is only then that the contemplative life blossoms, for the contemplative life must reach the Father, must reach what is ultimate in the mystery of God, that is, the divine secret of His fatherhood. Mary accepts to be enclosed in God in and through her act of contemplative faith. Throughout the history of the Church there have been recluses, hermits, that is, men and women consecrated to God who accept to be enclosed behind a wall completely. These exterior enclosures are but signs of the mystery of the "reclusion" of Christian faith which blossoms fully in the contemplative life which is lived in the mercy of the Father. It is the Father's mercy itself that encloses the human intellect rendering it totally "captive" to the divine, in order to enable it to live solely the gift that the Father gives of His Word, of His Son.

Divine Motherhood: Act of Hope

Mary's motherly cooperation with the gift of the Father occurs in faith, a faith which engages her whole life and plunges her into silence. It also occurs in hope.

Faith calls for hope and love. In the mystery of abandonment we saw that hope is based on the mercy of the Father. In the mystery of contemplation, hope is based on a promise, on the word of God which is a promise, the promise fulfilled in the gift of the Son. As long as the promise remains prophetic, as in the Old Testament, hope cannot be contemplative. Contemplative hope is based on the gift that the Father gives, that is, His Son, and therefore, on the promise already fulfilled in its substantial aspect. Of course hope is not yet complete possession. A sign of this is that the Father gives us His Son as a little child. That is why Mary's hope is motherly. Mary hopes as a mother hopes in her child. We indeed use the beautiful expression, "expecting a child." Expectation is hope. A mother hopes. Her heart hopes for her child because the child is the continuation of her life. A mother is, as it were, carried by her child. In Mary's heart, which receives the Father's gift, there is an analogous hope, a divine hope which is motherly because the Father gives her His Son with a promise, "He will reign over the house of Jacob forever and His kingdom will have no end."[115] The Father's merciful omnipotence is communicated to Mary in her Son. The Father's omnipotence is, as it were, given to Mary. The Father realizes His masterpiece of love in Mary with her cooperation. This masterpiece of the Father's merciful omnipotence is both the fruit, and the new means, the new source of Mary's hope, as the child is the hope of its mother. Mary has no other desire in her heart than to receive the Father's promise, the promise which is realized in her in this personal gift.

The contemplative hope of a Christian is based upon the merciful omnipotence of the Father who gives Himself entirely. Such hope can capture human ambition and desire to the extent these are human, for purely imaginary desire and false ambition cannot be assumed by theological hope. Everything must be surrendered entirely to the Father in and through the gift He gives. We must accept to cooperate with the promise and the gift with all our strength.

In her hope, Mary becomes the servant of God in an exceptional way. Is she not more of a servant than all the great servants of God in the Old Testament, more of a servant than even John the Baptist, the precursor? Faith and hope, which translate into her "fiat", engage her whole life and transform her into a servant. She was to cooperate with God's merciful omnipotence by becoming the mother of the Promise in her whole being. The

115. Lk 1:33

"substantial" Promise of the Father, the Word, our Savior, assumes flesh and blood from Mary and in Mary. Every act of Christian contemplation here on earth engages us in the service of God and calls us to cooperate with Him. Not only does God ask us to receive His light, but He also awaits our cooperation in the realization of His promise. Every act of Christian contemplation implies an intense desire (the desire of hope) to cooperate efficaciously and divinely in the reign of the Father through His Son, in this divine and temporal reign, by surrendering ourselves to the promise as though it could not be fulfilled without us. Christian contemplation necessarily implies that a Christian accept to be completely a servant of God, surrendering to Him all vital energy, all possibilities for conquest and domination. Contemplation that is limited to the peaks of the intellect would only be philosophical contemplation. Such contemplation implies no exterior service. Indeed, a philosopher does not seek only principles; he seeks to contemplate reality. Yet, even though through his contemplation the philosopher becomes the servant of the One he recognizes as the source of his being and life, his whole life is nevertheless not engaged in this service. Christian contemplation, however, implies total service of God, of the Father's gift. In the supernatural life a contemplative contemplates in receiving the Father's personal gift, in becoming all-welcoming, wholly receptive, actively and lovingly receptive vis-à-vis this gift. This receptivity mobilizes all his vital energy in the service of Christ. Far from dispensing from service, Christian contemplation demands it and enables it to reach its full dimension. Christian contemplation gives a Christian the possibility and the quality of a "useless servant."[116]

As mother, Mary becomes the servant par excellence. It is both in hope and in faith that she becomes a servant. Theological hope has a fundamental connection with the *mores* of the servants of God. Theological hope establishes a Christian as a servant of God in a very radical fashion, for it surrenders his life, his capacity to work, his efficacious power, to the

116. Lk 17:10

Father's merciful omnipotence. A person who hopes with supernatural hope knows that he does not save himself. He knows that his salvation is given to him gratuitously; but he also knows that this gratuitousness engages him more deeply than if salvation had come completely from him, for God saves as one saves a friend, asking that his friend cooperate. Is not a friend the most efficacious and the most devoted of servants?

The greatest service that exists is that of motherhood. It is the most engaging, the most sensitive, the most indispensable of services. Every other servant can be replaced. A mother cannot be replaced. A mother is irreplaceable precisely because her whole being is mother. Motherhood is not only a function or a job as is sometimes said today ("my job as mother"). Such expressions risk becoming somewhat inhumane, for being a mother is not a job. It is something much deeper as regards the heart, as regards sensitivity and affection, as regards a woman's whole life. The service of motherhood is a complete service, a service which takes hold of everything. Motherhood reduced to pure function loses its human quality. It becomes like that of animals. True human motherhood takes possession of the heart. It engages the whole person. That is why it is prolonged in the education of a child.

At the supernatural level, motherhood acquires an infinitely greater character. The realistic character of Mary's hope places her entirely at the service of God. Her hope takes hold of her whole being, making of her a true servant, a "little, useless, servant". Indeed, one must be little in service in order to be "useless". Uselessness depends upon littleness. It is in evangelical littleness that we discover and live such uselessness in service. We indeed see it in Mary. Accepting to be the mother of God includes this uselessness because it is accepting to have no rights over her son. Mary has no idea what this motherhood will be. Mothers can normally foresee and plan. Mary, the mother of God, becomes a mother in faith. She accepts not to be able to plan, not to know what God will ask of her, to entrust herself blindly to Him. She does pose one question, however. "How will it occur?" But the question does not express worry. It expresses a desire to enter fully into the will of her Lord. She desires to know how she can serve. And so the angel plunges her again into passiveness to help her to understand that she must accept this service in its totality, in obscurity, without seeking to understand what it will be. Mary accepts to be the mother of God as a useless servant, surrendering herself to all the demands of God's love.

Such is the realism of Christian hope. We often lack hope because we hope in an abstract fashion. We hope for "heaven," but a heaven often very distant. We forget that the Kingdom of God is "within us." Hope has to do with the Kingdom of God hidden within us. Hope has to do with Christ who has taken hold of us, and others, making of us His living members, and asking us that we serve Him in one another. As Mary was servant of the Head of the body, we are servants of the members of the Body. This teaches us practically and concretely what the Christian contemplative life is. The Christian life has deep, extraordinary realism. Not only is this life lived in acts of contemplation which bring to completion what is purest in the human intellect, but it must capture all our vital forces, that is, our sensitivity, our heart, and our capacity to work. Everything must be bound in hope and surrendered to the merciful omnipotence of the Father who gives Himself in and through His only Son. Evangelical littleness must reign in our inmost desires, our powers, our capacities, our will in order to purify our hope and transform it into an absolutely divine desire for the Father's love, for the ascendancy of the Father's gift, that is, the Son. This desire must be born of hope and must be only with respect to the Father's merciful and omnipotent will for us.

Here evangelical littleness is translated into the "uselessness" of service. Mary's hope allows her to live as a useless servant, as a servant who does not possess the gift of love given to her, but who receives it such that she is surrendered to it. In her childlike hope with regard to the gift of the Father, in her maternal hope with regard to the one to become her son, Mary declares herself, in all truthfulness, the "servant of the Lord." Under the guidance of the Holy Spirit, she understands that Christian hope must be brought to completion in an efficacious desire, a desire which is not a whim to accomplish something wonderful, a beautiful dream, but a deep desire to serve God as the One who must be "first served". When our hope is too "human", it easily becomes whim and daydream. It becomes tainted with imaginary things, as do idealized human desires, which become manifold and varied according to the fertility of the imagination. This human mode must be purified in order for hope to be strengthened. The Father's divine ambitions for us infinitely surpass anything that we can imagine. Let us not, under pretext of purifying human desire, fall into a sort of pusillanimity which leads to underestimating and even despising the Father's mercy. God's ambitions are those of an infinitely good father. He desires that His children be like Him. He desires to communicate His inheritance. To the extent that we are children of God, we are heirs (*si filii, et heredes*).[117] The inheritance of the Father is His Son. Christian hope leads us to desire that Jesus reign in us, as He reigns, in a certain sense, in the Father, for the Son "who is close beside the Father"[118] indeed reigns in the Father in that the Father "gives Him His glory".[119] Because of this glory he receives His kingdom from the Father.

The Father wishes for His Son to reign fully in us. Hope receives from the Father this promise as an efficacious promise, as a substantially fulfilled promise.[120] Even if we do not see it or observe it, the promise is already fulfilled in us. We must be "impoverished" regarding the promise in order to leave all the room for Christ's reign, for the Father's mercy communicated through the promise. Christian hope raises us to the level of divine ambition. As children of God, as those who receive everything from God, we must adopt the ambitions of our Father — as did Mary in the Annunciation. In

117. Rm 8:17; Gal 4:7
118. Jn 1:2, 8:38, 15:26
119. Jn 1:14, 8:54, 12:28, 17:5, 22, & 24
120. Cf. Heb 11:1; "faith is the substance of things hoped for…"

order for the divine mystery to take hold of everything in us, our desires must place us in an attitude of useless servants of God, and this demands great poverty.

Divine Motherhood: Act of Love

We only truly cooperate with a personal gift of love by means of a personal gift of love. Mary receives the Father's gift and cooperates with it in faith, in hope, through love and the gift of herself.

Mary's will is exercised in evangelical littleness which is only perfect in love, in love given in response to God's gift. Only giving to the one who gives himself can bring about true littleness. Mary's will was entirely taken by and submitted to the love of God and so evangelical littleness comes about in her heart. Is evangelical littleness not the fundamental receptivity of charity as it stands before the greatness of God's love? Does not evangelical littleness express the special depth of the soul as it loves God supernaturally, a depth which has the soul, as it were, disappear in order to yield to the Beloved, to the One who is Love? Once a person grasps that he gives himself to One who loved him first [121] (because He is Love, the Source of all love, of all gift, because He is the only one who can teach us how to love), immediately littleness becomes the only real interior attitude. Such littleness in love gives to a Christian the sense of his radical incapacity to love God as God ought to be loved with all the qualities of love, with pure, disinterested generosity, with complete transparency, with no self-centeredness. We must love God as He loves us. The human heart, however, is incapable, by itself, of such simplicity, of such purity of love. When grasped with acuteness, this incapacity places us in a state of littleness, of radical humility. For, if we are incapable of loving, we can do nothing. Indeed, supernatural love gives our life its meaning and eternal value.

In the human person we must distinguish between the love of concupiscence and the love of friendship. Thomas Aquinas

---

121. 1 Jn 4:19

Aquinas makes this distinction, in the footsteps of Aristotle. The love of concupiscence draws us to what is inferior. It inclines downward. It does not have us love the other for itself, but for us. If we love good wine, for example, it is not at all for the wine itself, but for us. We love good wine because it tastes good, because it pleases us. Is this not often how we love? The love of concupiscence is very fundamental in us. It takes root in our vegetative life and is the normal appetite of our sensitive life. Because it is rooted especially in the vegetative life, it tends towards possession, and very often corrupts, degrades the love of friendship. The love of friendship ought to be spiritual, gratuitous, and generous. Humanly speaking, the love of friendship is rare, whereas the love of concupiscence is widespread and common. The love of concupiscence takes root in us, often penetrating our inmost generous movements of spiritual love to diminish and stain them and sometimes paralyze and kill them. In such conditions, because it is rooted in poor human hearts filled with concupiscence, human friendship, instead of being spiritual, is filled with desires for possession. We say that we love our friends for themselves and indeed desire to do so; yet there is often a secret desire to possess others and draw them to ourself.

When grace, when charity, fully penetrates the heart, it purifies it radically and completely. This we can contemplate in Mary. In her, grace truly and completely penetrated. There is no trace of concupiscence. Everything in her is "absorbed" by charity which blossoms into evangelical littleness, enabling her to give herself totally, to forget herself completely, to consider only the Father's gift: His Son. Her disinterested and generous and tender love opens the living forces of her heart. There was no human heart more blossomed than that of Mary at the Annunciation. Mary loves as a "daughter of God". In God, there is only pure, absolute selfless love: The Father gives Himself totally to His Son. Because Mary is little and has completely abandoned herself, she can thus have a love similar to that of the Father for His Son – at least to the extent it is possible for a creature. In this [selfless] love, Mary comes out of herself completely and forgets herself in order to move towards the one who gives Himself and to belong only to Him. Mary's pure love surrenders her to the gift of God. It enables her heart to beat in unison with the heart of Jesus, the Son of the Father and her own son, in perfect unity.

Except when it seizes us very intimately, the love of God is often intermingled with a lot of human "junk" from which we have a difficult time freeing ourselves. We will never succeed by ourselves in reaching the Father's love. The love of concupiscence crushes us. We have to ask the Father, and Mary herself, to help us to understand from within the quality of the love which she has, she who is "mother of fairest love".[122] The Father willed in the mystery of the Annunciation that her love as child be so pure that it become maternal. Let us ask Mary to give us this all-pure openess so that we might finally forget ourselves completely, so that we might rid ourselves of the habit of constantly turning in on ourselves, of always "looking in the mirror". Such habits weigh so heavily upon love. The moment we finish doing a generous deed, we ponder the satisfaction it brings. Let us contemplate in Mary the love of a child running to encounter its father. Mary lives a plenitude of love. The purity of her faith and the poverty of her hope are at the service of this virginal gift whereby her whole heart is surrendered to the Father's gift.

For the human psyche, the two are distinct: a child is other than a mother. In Mary's heart, however, these two coincide. One must be "little" in order to become maternal with respect to God. One must be in a state of absolute, evangelical littleness, in a state of nakedness and loving disinterest with respect to self, in order to receive the Father's gift. God cannot give Himself to someone who is not poor, to someone who grabs what is given to him. The moment our heart begins to grab and possess, the moment our love is not sufficiently pure, selfless, stripped and generous, oneness with God cannot come about. Now, if the Father gives us His Son, it is so that we might

---

122. Sir 24:24

become sons and daughters. John says that those who have received the light have received "the power to become children of God."[123] And because there is only one Son, if we give ourselves completely to Jesus, we ought to become one with him.

For there to be such oneness, the profound unity of love is essential. In order to give ourselves completely to the Father through the Son, the Son must take complete possession of us, such that, with Him, we have one desire, one love, one will. Mary's "fiat" translates this extremely simple attitude. The motherly fiat of the Father's little child, as well as her attitude as servant express it, for faith engages her whole life in the service of God. Mary must serve the Light of the Father. Hope engages her in this poor, "useless", maternal service, whereas, thanks to love, she becomes a gift to the Father, not only in the peaks of her intellect and heart, but in all that she is.

Christian Contemplation and Maternal Service: Poverty of a Servant

Mary, a little child of God, accepts to be Mother, to be servant of God. Her motherhood, which is to become the form of her contemplation, implies littleness and the state of a useless servant. Her contemplation implies a very intimate gift of herself. It implies the divine exercise of faith, hope and love which captivate her intellect and will and place her interiorly at the service of God. At the same time, her contemplation directly and essentially translates into maternal service. Her faith, hope and love imply, therefore, a wonderful orientation for her human life.

As distinguished from philosophical contemplation, Christian contemplation seizes a whole human life. Philosophical contemplation occurs in the peaks of the intellect and perfects what is purest in it. According to Aristotle, contemplation is the most perfect happiness. According to him, all the necessities of life, human life *per se*, human virtue, are dispositions towards this perfect happiness. He tends to eliminate, as much as possible, any contradictions or human difficulties for the sake of this

___

123. Jn 1:12

happiness, of this contemplative gaze, thus enclosing himself in an "ivory tower". When God himself wished to plant the contemplative life on earth, He did not choose a philosopher. He planted it in the heart of a mother. He took the heart of a little child and made it the heart of a mother. Mary's whole life was seized. The peaks of her intellect accepted to be silent so that love could take everything. Indeed, love took all her vital forces: those of her heart, her faculties, her sensitivity. Mary's whole life was, as it were, "assumed" and placed at the service of the Father.

The service of God is part of the contemplative life. One cannot be contemplative here on earth without mobilizing his strength for the service of God. To claim that contemplation is limited to the peaks of the intellect and that the rest is for the active life is not to understand Christian contemplation and to return to that of the philosopher. The mystery of the Annunciation precisely teaches us that the attitude of the useless, little servant allows unity between contemplation and the service of God. The mystery of the Presentation is, as it were, the foundation of this attitude. Mary surrenders completely to God as His little child. That is why she can receive His treasure with absolute simplicity. And because she received it with such purity, her whole life was placed at the service of God. In Mary we see a child placing all the strength of her humanness at the service of God. The uselessness of her service, the poverty of her attitude flow from the child-like quality she has.

At the Annunciation Mary's heart must live this deep demand for poverty so that the service of her motherhood will not be opposed to the contemplative attitude of a child receiving the Father's gift. Indeed, from a psychological viewpoint there is no clearer opposition than that between the contemplative attitude and the maternal attitude. Human motherhood necessarily implies an active life, implies activity. Motherhood is the most engaging and demanding service. Human motherhood takes hold of everything in a woman, and it deeply blossoms her human life. Contemplation, on the contrary, normally demands solitude, great passiveness and a certain progressive separation in order to gaze only upon God and receive only Him. A mother finds herself in a family, and thus, in the heaviest, most rooted and also the most stable human community. The contemplative life calls for solitude and detachment.

God disposed all things in the supernatural realm so that these two realities be divinely surpassed in Mary, in the mystery of her divine motherhood. Mary is the contemplative woman *par excellence*, vowed to God, gazing upon Him in extraordinary solitude, in reclusion. At the same time, God awaits of her the service of motherhood in a perfect fashion. Mary is more "mother" than any other mother. Her motherhood is miraculous. Her motherhood "exploits" in her, more deeply than in any other woman, all the riches of humanness — but without detracting from her contemplation. The two demands are united in her. They are not opposed because her maternal service is lived in total divine poverty and in no way stains the purity of her heart. Not only are contemplation and motherhood not opposed in her, but Mary's maternal service enables her contemplation to be deeper, and more present, and to radiate in the whole of her life. Thanks to this service, Mary experiences a more complete contemplation, towards which she is moved from the depths of who she is. Everything in Mary is turned towards God. Her child is her God, and the more her child is rooted in her, the more he takes hold of her vital forces, and the more Mary is turned towards God.

Do we not have a model and example here which enables us to unify the oppositions that we often find in our lives? It is true that the Christian contemplative life entails certain activities which, as regards our psyche, do not lead us essentially towards contemplation. These activities include those with a view to the acquisition of virtue or to the fabrication of works, those activities which are result-oriented. Such activities are work, be they bodily or intellectual. Now, all work involves a certain temporal orientation, for all work seeks to be efficient, even those which are to acquire intellectual virtue or disposition or aptitudes. All work is part of the active life, and therefore, initially opposed to the receptivity characteristic of the contemplation of the children of God, initially opposed to the evangelical littleness that the gift of God necessitates.

The mystery of the Annunciation teaches us that there is no contemplative life here on earth without a certain service. This is how the contemplative life began in the Church and this is how it will continue. Work well done is valuable as regards the "regulation" of our sensitivity. This is only normal, for work puts our feet back on the ground. Work contributes to balance regarding our imagination. Work well done engages our sensitivity and our body. Work accomplished in conformity with God's will, in a certain sense, allows God to assume, or take hold, of everything in our human life. Through such work everything can become part of the temporal reign of God. Through such work the contemplative life can immediately radiate.

We are servants of God and we have a task to accomplish. As servants we must be attentive to this. This sometimes demands of us great efforts at attentiveness which can sometimes have us psychologically (though not deeply) abandon expectation and receptivity. All of this is part of God's will. In order to accomplish with the greatest possible attentiveness the service He asks of us, we must make this effort. A servant is assiduous in his task and God expects that he be faithful and meek. A servant who accomplishes his task with perfect attentiveness is faithful. A servant who accomplishes his task with graciousness and gentleness is meek. Let us add to these two qualities that which the New Testament demands: *uselessness*. This is demanded of all Christians. As long as a Christian has not reached this poverty, there remains a duality in his life. He is, as it were, torn between the duty of a servant and the attitude of a child of God in prayer. As long as a Christian has not reached this poverty, he stays at a predominantly psychological level and does not reach the height of faith. Consequently and inevitably, he allows himself to be overwhelmed by work or he maintains a very "human" nostalgia as regards prayer. To reduce the "competition", to reduce this duality between servant and little child thirsting for the contemplative life, one must be a "useless servant". The great secret resides in absolute poverty which inclines a person to the accomplishment of God's will rather than the realization of the work itself. In such poverty we do not seek to take possession of the work asked of us as though it were our own. We do not seek to do it because it pleases us, but to do it divinely, that is, because God asks it of us. We seek to do it for Him, as best we can, as Mary did all things. Such poverty alone can eliminate any opposition between servant and little child of God.

We can easily say, "It is impossible for me to live the contemplative life, to live an interior life. I have too much to do. I have too much work and it diminishes the intensity of my Christian life." Such reasoning is very human. We often hear complaints along these lines, especially today where the work to be done is increasing to the point of becoming unbearable. It is true that much work renders the contemplative life difficult. But the question does not lie there. The real question is whether or not God wants us to do the work, and how He wants it done. Even when willed by God, work done in a possessive spirit, impedes us from loving God freely and from being faithful to an authentic search for the contemplative life. We are the ones who create obstacles because of our possessiveness. The way we work keeps us from being totally surrendered to God. Who knows, perhaps, out of mercy, God has given us work that we might move this body of ours which needs exercise. Thanks to work, our hands, our feet, our senses, can be exercised in a useful way and can glorify God. Without work we risk useless restlessness. Through work, humbly and generously accepted, God Himself can take hold of our vital energy, can take hold of our need for activity as he took hold of the flesh, blood and vital energy in Mary in the mystery of the Incarnation. The "work" of Mary's motherhood is assumed for the glory of the Father. As mother of the Word made flesh, Mary glorifies the Father.

Work accomplished in a spirit of poverty and littleness, as stated before, is valuable for the equilibrium and purification of our sensitivity. Such work is connatural to our humanness and obliges us to have our feet on the ground, and be in touch. Such work safeguards the equilibrium of our imagination. Our body and our sensitivity are progressively educated through work, if it is done well. It is *really* done well when accomplished for God who wishes to take hold of everything in us, in conformity with His will. Through such work the temporal reign of Christ comes about. Through work, the contemplative life, the love of God, immediately radiate.

Poverty is the hinge that maintains unity. Without poverty, we risk letting ourselves be invaded by the frenzy of work, with a more or less conscious desire to let it be known that we are the one doing everything: "What would happen if I were not here?!" This temptation haunts those with an active and generous temperament. The other extreme is the risk of being taken with a certain disdain for work, considering work with condescension. We think we have a temperament which lends itself to contemplation. We may have received insights as regards the primacy of contemplation. But if we lack poverty, we easily fall into disdain for work. Such disdain cannot exist in Christian contemplation, for Christian contemplation implies a total service. The more we are children of God, the more we are servants: faithful, meek, poor and useless servants. One of the tangible signs of a lack of poverty is such thoughts (of personal indispensability or of disdain for work). If we discover such thoughts in ourselves, it is that we are not sufficiently poor. Because of the characteristic demands of contemplation and those of service, we may experience in ourselves a certain psychological duality. This is not surprising. As long as we are here on earth (*in via*), we will experience it. In fact. the more we progress and the more faithful we are, the more we will experience it. Even for a faithful and poor servant this opposition remains; but it is immediately surpassed, for a true servant understands that the best disposition to prayer, to contemplation, is to be attentive to the Father's mercy and love, no matter how they are given.

We can only live the mystery of God and contemplate Him by receiving His love. We do not pray by ourselves. It is by the grace of God that we pray. It is the Father who gives us His Son and who asks us to receive Him and live in and through Him. Now, being a servant of God is, above all, to receive the precepts of God and to accomplish them faithfully for Him. In our inmost selves, there is a deep unity between the attitude of servant and the attitude of the contemplative, attitudes which are, once again, psychologically diverse. Both are ordered to the Father. Both demand His intimate presence. That is why, in the midst of intense work, we can sometimes experience great intimacy with God, in extraordinary silence. Mary is present to our work, giving us Jesus. Mary is always present to give us Jesus. Consequently, the work of Nazareth, both demanding and gentle work, continues in the Church. Mary teaches us to work as she did, even if we are not always conscious of it. The deep and voluntary adherence to God's good will and pleasure remains and intensifies, demanding increasing spiritual poverty. This adherence truly stabilizes us in God, in His love and in His will.

Moses at Horeb, Mary at Nazareth

In order to penetrate the divine grandeur of the mystery of the Annunciation, it is good to consider its prefigurations in the Old Testament.[124] Let us consider here in a particular way the vocation of Moses, his vocation as a servant of God in the episode of the burning bush, which is an "annunciation" which

---

124. All of the annunciations of the Old Testament prefigure in a certain sense this unique and singular Annunciation. We must come back to them often in order to better understand the power of the angel's message in the Gospel of Luke. There were annunciations to Abraham (Gn 15, Gn 17:1-22, Gn 18:1-15), to Moses (Ex 3:1-22, Ex 4:1-17, Ex 19:1-25), to Gideon (Jgs 6:11-24) and to the mother of Samson (Jgs 13:2-24). These, however, only prefigure the mystery of the Annunciation to Mary. We must not use them therefore to explain the latter. On the contrary, the New Testament sheds the ultimate light for a Christian. The less perfect is always explained by the more perfect.

prefigures that of Mary and which both resembles it and differs from it.

Let us first note the stripped, simple character of the passage in Luke's Gospel as compared to the text from Exodus. We know very little of the historical, geographic and human circumstances of the Annunciation to Mary, such as date and place. Luke maintains great discretion, prompted no doubt by Mary's discretion. Different artists have tried to imagine the dialogue. Such efforts are legitimate, but, for a believer, seeking to be educated by Mary, the poverty of detail is, as it were, an invitation to consider only the mystery. The mystery alone is what counts. For Mary, this mystery is, above all, that of the personal gift of the Son given by the Father. In her Annunciation, Mary is above all she who receives the Father's gift and who is perfectly possessed by it; she who bears the gift by receiving it in faith and by enveloping it maternally and who, at the same time, is borne by the gift and enveloped by it. The gift transforms her life. The gift is a source of life for her.

The annunciations in the Old Testament and the passage in Exodus, that of the burning bush in particular, are much richer in detail. The Old Testament is always more descriptive. It better expresses psychical and human attitudes. It is more educational. In the passage which concerns us here, we see how a servant must receive God's will and how he must make it his own. God's will gives him greater strength and greater efficiency, for he no longer acts on his own behalf, but on behalf of Yahweh. The Gospel of Luke presents, above all, the attitude of a little child who believes in the words of its Father. God certainly expresses His will and demands a service, but it is a service of love which must flow from the heart of a child and express a superabundance of love as its fruit. The service of motherhood flows from Mary's heart as an irradiation of her contemplation, whereas Moses was not yet a contemplative when God asked of him his mission. Moses lived as a just man, desirous of respecting justice; and it was with this attitude that he received God's will, that he accepted his vocation. Moses is an excellent servant of God. He is just and prudent (he flees when he discovers Pharaoh is pursuing him). He is just and prudent like Zechariah. Let us read these beautiful texts from Exodus to discover how God forms His servant.

Now Moses was keeping the flock of his father-in-law, Jethro, the priest of Midian; and he led his flock to the west side of the wilderness, and came to Horeb, the mountain of God. And the angel of the Lord appeared to him in a flame of fire from the midst of a bush; and he looked, and lo, the bush was burning, yet it was not consumed. And Moses said, "I will turn aside and see this great sight why the bush is not burnt." When the Lord saw that he turned aside to see, God called to him from the bush, "Moses, Moses!" And he said, "Here am I." Then he said, "Do not come near; remove your shoes from your feet, for the place on which you are standing is holy ground." And he said, "I am the God of your fathers, the God of Abraham, the God of Isaac, and the God of Jacob." And Moses hid his face, for he was afraid to look at God.

Then the Lord said, "I have seen the affliction of my people who are in Egypt, and have heard their cry because of their taskmasters; I know their sufferings, and I have come down to deliver them from the hand of the Egyptians, and to bring them forth from that land to a good and broad land, a land flowing with milk and honey, to a place of the Canaanites, the Hittites, the Amorites, the Perizzites, the Hivites, and the Jebusites. And now, behold, the cry of the people of Israel has come to me, and I have seen the oppression with which the Egyptians oppress them. Come, I will send you to Pharaoh that you may bring forth my people, the sons of Israel, out of Egypt." But Moses said to God, "Who am I that I should go to Pharaoh, and bring the sons of Israel out of Egypt?'" He said, "but I will be with you; and this shall be the sign for you, that I have sent you: when you have brought forth the people from Egypt, you shall serve God upon this mountain."

Then Moses said to God, "If I come to the people of Israel and say to them, 'the God of your fathers has sent me to you,' and they ask me, 'What is his name?' what shall I say to them?" God said to Moses, "I AM WHO AM." And he said, "Say this to the people of Israel, 'I AM has sent me to you.'" God also said to Moses, "Say this to the people of Israel, 'The Lord, the God of your fathers, The God of Abraham, the God of Isaac, and the God of Jacob, has sent me to you': this is my name forever, and thus I am to be remembered throughout all generations. Go and gather the elders of Israel together, and say to them, 'The Lord, The God of your fathers, the God of Abraham, of Isaac, and of Jacob, has appeared to me, saying, 'I have observed you and what has been done to you in Egypt; and I promise that I will bring you forth from the affliction of Egypt, to the land of the Canaanites, the Hittites, the Amorites, the Perizzites, the Hivites, and the Jebusites, a land flowing with milk and honey.' And they will hearken to your voice, and you and the elders of Israel shall go to the king of Egypt and say to him, 'The Lord, the God of the Hebrews, has met with us; and now, we pray you, let us go a three days' journey into the wilderness, that we may sacrifice to the Lord our God.' I know that the king of Egypt will not let you go unless compelled by a mighty hand. So I will stretch out my hand and smite Egypt with all the wonders which I will do in it; after that he will let you go. And I will give this people favor in the sight of the Egyptians; and when you go, you shall not go empty, but each woman shall ask of her neighbor, and of her who sojourns in her house, jewelry of silver and of gold, and clothing, and you shall put them on your sons and on your daughters; thus you shall despoil the Egyptians."

Then Moses answered, "But, behold, they will not believe me or listen to my voice, for they will say, 'The Lord did not appear to you.'" The Lord said to him, "what is that in your hand?" He said, "A rod." And he said, "Cast it on the ground." So he cast it on the ground, and it became a serpent; and Moses fled from it. But the Lord said to Moses, "Extend your hand and take it by the tail" — so he extended his hand and caught it, and it became a rod in his hand — "that they may believe that the Lord, the God of their fathers, the God of Abraham, the God of Isaac, and the God of Jacob, has appeared to you." Again, the Lord said to him, "Put your hand into your bosom." And he put his hand into his bosom; and when he took it out, behold, his hand was leprous, as white as snow. The God said, "Put your hand back into your bosom." So he put his hand back into his bosom; and when he took it out, behold, it was restored like the rest of his flesh. "If they will not believe you," God said, "or heed the first sign, they may believe the latter sign. If they do not believe even these two signs or heed your voice, you shall take some water from the Nile and pour it upon the dry ground; and the water which you shall take from the Nile shall become blood upon the dry ground."

But Moses said to the Lord, "Oh, my Lord, I am not eloquent, either heretofore or since thou hast spoken to thy servant; but I am slow of speech and of tongue." Then the Lord said to him, "Who hast made man's mouth? Who makes him dumb or deaf, or seeing or blind? Is it not I, the Lord? Now therefore go, and I will be with your mouth and teach you what you shall speak." But he said, "Oh, my Lord, send, I pray, some other person." Then the anger of the Lord was kindled against Moses and he said, "Is there not Aaron, your brother, the Levite? I know that he can speak well; and behold, he is coming out to meet you, and when he sees you he will be glad in his heart. And you shall speak to him and put the words in his mouth; and I will be with your mouth and with his mouth, and will teach you what you shall do. He shall speak for you to the people; and he shall be a mouth for you, and you shall be to him as God. And you shall take in your hand this rod, with which you shall do the signs."[125]

This text is indeed the great revelation of God's mercy for His people. It is God the Savior who reveals Himself, as He does later to Mary. Is "Jesus" not the name to be given to the Son of the Most High? There is a wonderful parallelism between these two annunciations. On the one hand, God stoops to take His people from the hands of Pharaoh; and on the other hand, God stoops to humanity to give it its Savior. However, we must note the distance between these two great revelations of God's mercy.

In the beautiful passage from Exodus we discover the merciful heart of the Father, "I have witnessed the affliction of my people and have heard their cry. I know well what they are suffering; therefore, I have come to rescue them." Knowledge of affliction and deep resolution to rescue are indeed the main elements of mercy. God wishes to save his people, to withdraw them from affliction and lead them to a land flowing with milk and honey. We are indeed in the presence of a great revelation of the mercy of God to His servant, but this revelation occurs in a different fashion from that of the mystery of the Annunciation. Moses is still only a servant. He ignores what contemplation is, what the mountain of God is: Horeb, the burning bush, and the flame of fire which comes forth from it. He senses that it is an awesome place and can only be approached with a distant, religious attitude. God obliges him to remove his sandals. At the Annunciation, the "burning bush" and the "flame of fire" are in Mary. She is the "mountain of God". In God's little child comes forth the burning bush and its flame, and from within it God calls her. He greets her through the mediation of the angel, but from within. Did the angel present himself to Mary externally as we most often imagine it? More than likely, but the reality resides in Mary. Everything occurs in Mary's burning heart. The greatness of the Annunciation is not found in its external symbols, but in the burning fire which, from Mary's heart, rises to meet the Father.

Moses the servant does not yet enter into intimacy with God.

125. Ex 3:1-22; 4:1-17

The revelation at Horeb is a revelation of mercy given above all to the servant. The burning bush, in which God is manifested, is exterior to Moses and Moses, seized with fear and admiration, veils his face. A beloved child of God does not see his Father, but in the obscurity of faith, fixes his gaze upon Him. Even if, as certain theologians claim, at the moment of the Annunciation, Mary enjoyed a glimpse of the Beatific Vision (*per modum transeuntis*), her interior attitude is the same. A little child of the Father, be it in the Beatific Vision or in pure faith, stands before the Father and adheres to Him face-to-face in mutual and complete love — either in luminosity or in obscurity. A servant cannot gaze upon God. Moses hides and veils his face, "for he was afraid to look at God," as the Book of Exodus says. This is indeed the attitude of the virtue of religion. The virtue of religion gives a very acute sense of the Creator, omnipotent and actively present in our inmost selves, before whom the only possible act is an act of adoration. Adoration was indeed Moses' act before the burning bush. And God manifested His mercy from within the bush just as the angel speaks to announce the new mercy of the Father, in Mary's inmost heart.

The story of Moses gives us a description. It is thereby closer to us, and yet it is less deep as regards the revelation of mercy. Moses listens, but does not understand very well. The servant, the "old man," never understands mercy very well. The child understands it spontaneously. Moses is fearful and his first attitude is withdrawal, "Who am I that I should go to Pharaoh and lead the Israelites out of Egypt?" Moses is not aware of this extraordinary thing: mercy! He is thinking only about himself, "who am I," turning in on himself, as a servant has recourse to prudence. Each time God speaks to him of Pharaoh, Moses, as a servant respectful of authority, becomes fearful and turns in on himself. Hence God, overflowing with mercy, not only for His people, but for this poor, trembling servant, assures Moses, "I will be with you." And yet this does not suffice for this prudent and tenacious Moses. But, "When I go to the Israelites and say to them, 'The God of your fathers has sent me to you,' if they ask me, 'What is His name?'" Imagine the audacity of this servant asking God His name. The patriarchs never did it, for they were friends of God. God immediately called them His friends. When we are someone's friend, we do not need to know his name, for we know him from within. We ask the name of someone who is unknown, who is a stranger. A name is a sort of badge or label, which allows us to find more easily the person we are seeking. A name remains exterior to the person. We have no need to know the name of a person we know from within. The servant asked God His name precisely because he did not yet know Him from within, intimately. God had revealed to him His mercy and had assured him of His intimate presence, "I will be with you," and yet Moses did not understand. This intimate presence of God, however, was presence to a servant, not to a friend. With the presence of "immensity" as theologians call it, that is, the presence of the Creator to its creature, God is indeed present to His creature but the creature is not present to God. The creature does not experience God. God thus remains enigmatic and distant. The creature does not know God's name. As a servant, the creature needs to know God's name in order to lean upon Him. Moses requests this. He requests an authority that he can present to others and say, "I am sent by the one who bears this name."

The way in which God names Himself for His servant is the great revelation of God as Creator. The name given by God is not His intimate name. The name "God is love" is transmitted later, by John. It was necessary that Mary teach John this name, for John translates in his Gospel, as a theologian, what Mary lived. At Horeb, God reveals His name as Creator, "I Am Who Am," the Lord of all. Everything comes from God and, consequently, everything that exists bears a reflection of Him. God is the only one who can name Himself in this way. It is not a philosophical knowledge of the being of God, but truly a divine and direct knowledge. The proof is that God reveals Himself to

Moses in a dialogue. Moses has an experience of God the Creator that the philosopher *per se* does not have. A servant can only be docile and faithful to the extent that he experientially knows he is serving the one named, "Who Am." This name must be inscribed in our will and our intellect so that we might be able to lean upon the authority of God the Creator and avoid the temptations of a servant's rebellion. In the Hebrew text, the word "servant" is much stronger than in today's language. For the author of the text, "servant" is actually "slave." If a servant wishes to be a slave, he has need of an authority, for a slave entrusts himself completely to the authority whom he serves.

"Who Am" is thus the name God communicated to Moses, a name different than the intimate name to be an object of contemplation, to be known in an act of love. These two names are two great revelations which we must compare and consider in parallel if we are to understand their unity. What dominates the Old Testament is the revelation of God's name to Moses. What dominates the New Testament, or rather what begins the New Testament, is the Annunciation to Mary in which the name of Jesus is revealed to us. It was not the name of the Father that was revealed to Mary. She had no need of that revelation. As His beloved little child, she knew it. She remained hidden in the Father and He entirely in her. The Father names Jesus so that we might understand the great role of the Savior. The salvation which Jesus brings to us is fulfilled in the deep oneness of life which Mary immediately lived in her Annunciation.

These two great revelations complement one another. Indeed, the intimate mystery of God always implies the mystery of the Creator. In other words, the Old Testament does not disappear. The intimate revelation of the Father to Mary implies the revelation of the Creator, and surpasses it. When announcing the Passion and the Cross Jesus says, "When you lift up the Son of Man then you will realize that I Am,"[126] a statement which recalls the revelation of God to Moses. Jesus was speaking officially to His friends and servants, and to His enemies, indeed, to the entire

126. Jn 8:28

world. At the Cross, Jesus perfectly fulfills the great revelation of the Annunciation and the great revelation of Horeb. At the Cross, Jesus has Mary enter more intimately than ever into the Father's love. Jesus crucified teaches Mary, and teaches us, that love is stronger than death, stronger than the deadly wound in His heart, stronger than anything. He teaches us that love surpasses everything. The wound in Jesus' heart is the ultimate revelation of the Father's love for Mary, for His friends. Although the revelation occurs officially before everyone, only friends understand. For the rest, the revelation occurs in exterior manifestations: the earthquake, the darkness, the tearing of the temple veil... powerful exterior manifestations which, in a certain sense, reproduce, at Calvary, the atmosphere of the burning bush. God manifests Himself as the Creator, as Almighty. He shows that He is truly present in His Son, that He is one with Him: "Truly this was the Son of God."[127]

The two revelations of God-Creator and God-love are therefore found in the mystery of the Cross. To Mary, to the child, God reveals His fatherly love in silence. The Father has no need to say His name to His child. To humanity who must serve its God, who must rediscover a sense of God's divine transcendence, who must know its Master both as Creator and Love, He reveals His loving omnipotence. And because these two aspects are part of the very mystery of God, they are necessarily linked to our contemplative life.

Education of A Servant

" 'I Am Who Am': this is what you shall tell the Israelites, 'I Am' sent me to you." "I Am" means the Absolute One. God thereby reveals His transcendence. God alone can name Himself such, for He alone *is* in His entire being. The revelation is very personal. God does not make Himself known philosophically (universally). He reveals His very person as Creator, a Being subsistent in Himself who is absolutely simple: *I Am*. In His entire being *He Is*. He is the one whose name is: *I Am*.

---

127. Mt 27:54

The servant of God is thus accompanied by the transcendence of God who lives in him. " 'I Am' sent me to you." A servant *per se* understands with difficulty God's absolute authority. The Scripture text here manifests it and thereby indicates how difficult it is to have a sense of God when we do not enter the contemplative life. Moses is not just anybody. He has a certain stature and a very strong personality. He was chosen by God. He is just and prudent, and yet he experiences great difficulty in grasping this revelation of God. He still lacks divine strength which leans only on the authority of God. Out of mercy, God sustains his faith with signs. The active life which we continue to live and which must increasingly serve God, has need of signs. God gives signs to the servant, not to the child, for God wants there to be only love for the child, without distraction. Signs would be a distraction for the child.

God gives Moses three beautiful signs which manifest the connection between the mystery of the burning bush and the mystery of the Cross. The three signs are, in fact, relative to the Cross. The first sign is the staff transformed into a serpent, which announces the sign later given in the desert: the bronze serpent attached to the wood which prefigures the crucified One. Humanity is symbolized by the wood. The serpent bears a twofold symbolism. 1) The serpent is the Devil, insofar as he is the Prince of lies. (A serpent is a cunning animal which deceives.) 2) The serpent is Jesus insofar as He wishes to descend as low as sinners. Psalm 22:7 can apply to Jesus, "I am a worm, not a man." The scorn of men. The wood was changed into a serpent and the serpent into wood. The Cross shows us Jesus attached to the wood, Jesus annihilated, Jesus as a "worm", attached to the wood which symbolizes humanity, the spouse of Christ. In this light we understand the meaning of the first sign given by God to Moses out of mercy. The merciful act of God, saving His people from the hands of Pharaoh, only prefigures another mercy. The changing of the wood into the serpent leads us to understand that the omnipotence of God is at the service of His love.

The second sign, the leprous hand, has a similar but inverse meaning. The wood was changed into a serpent. On the Cross, humanity is transformed by Jesus into a child of God. But for this to occur the humanity of Jesus without blemish, which bears the iniquity of the world, must become, as it were, "leprous", as did the hand of Moses when he put it in his bosom. When humanity turns in on itself, it becomes leprous. Jesus bore the iniquity of the world, the impurity of humanity, in order to render it its purity.

The third sign, the water changed into blood, is given out of superabundance, and also announces what is to happen at the Cross. The water changed into blood, as the water changed into wine at Cana, is prefigurative of the mystery of the Cross. Our human heart, as the heart of a servant and no more, is filled with stagnant water which can poison. In order for our heart to flow with living water, with the Holy Spirit, with Love, it must be transformed by the blood, by the heart of Jesus. This third sign manifests the plenitude of the Father's merciful act. God wishes to save His people from the hands of Pharaoh, a prefiguration of the great salvation to be wrought at the Cross.

And Moses, the faithful servant, does not yet understand! How much we resemble him. God gives us so many signs during the course of our life. They are perhaps not "staffs changed into serpents." They are, in fact, signs even more real, which lead us further. How many times has He healed our leprous soul? How many times has He transformed the bitter water of our hearts? How many times has He changed the sinner in us, the "old man," into a pure and loving child of God? And yet we still do not understand.

"Excuse me, my lord." Moses is fearful. He turns in on himself, whereas he ought simply to abandon himself to mercy, receive the word of God and let himself be transformed by it. "Excuse me, my Lord. I have not been eloquent heretofore, not even since you addressed Your words to Your servant." Moses is almost impolite. He wants God to improve him immediately, to give him a more eloquent tongue. Moses maintains his common sense, a sense which, in this case, is opposed to divine sense. He turns in on himself and perceives that his speech is awkward. He compares the mission God has entrusted to him with the qualities he possesses. How often we do this almost instinctively. We establish a parallel between our qualities, our faults, our inadequacies, and what God is asking of us. Moses says that it is impossible, and so God gives him a good lesson. The three signs were destined to strengthen his faith. Here we have the education of his hope. Because he is fearful, God shows him how to strengthen his hope. God gives him the formal motive for hope: the omnipotence and mercy of God. "Who gives one man speech and makes another deaf or dumb? Go then. It is I who will assist you and teach you what you are to say." God makes an imperative statement.

This, however, does not seem to suffice. Moses replies, "If you please, Lord, send someone else." In other words, "Leave me alone. I do not want to." When we lack love, we become cowardly. God then tries Moses. He wants to make of him a faithful servant, that is, a servant generous in love. God becomes "irritated" because Moses' resistance affects love. God can tolerate weaknesses with respect to faith and hope. He never tolerates, however, those with respect to love. The Devil always follows the same strategy. He seeks to make us fall first with respect to faith, then with respect to hope. But he never directly attacks love, for he knows not what love is. He has lost the sense of love. In this passage from Exodus the three great temptations of a servant are described. How God educates a servant to lead him to complete generosity is also described. God responds to Moses' lack of love in a magnificent way, with extraordinary magnanimity. The servant can do all he wants to create difficulty for God. God remains with him. "I will be with you." In order to overcome Moses' resistance, God does something even greater and more beautiful. He uses the lack of love to have His mercy overflow. He brings together His servants Moses and Aaron. God uses Moses' very weakness to place at his side someone who is to be, as it were, his "mouthpiece." He does this to be merciful also to Aaron, for God, as Thomas Aquinas says, "likes to multiply His instruments in order to have His mercy overflow."

There is a parallel between Moses and Aaron on one hand, and Mary and Joseph on the other. The two unions are very different, but there is a parallelism. God united Mary and Joseph in an extremely intimate fashion. Joseph is the spouse and guardian of Mary. He hides her and is, in a certain sense, her spokesman. Mary is silent and when she must speak she refers to his authority. For Joseph, Mary is like God, for God is given to Joseph in her. She is the living tabernacle of God for him. When he wonders whether or not he must divorce her, God orders him to take her more deeply, more completely, as he would take his God. "What has been conceived in her is of the Holy Spirit."[128] This something of God is God Himself. The union between Mary and Joseph is prefigured beautifully by the manner in which God gives Aaron to Moses. Moses fears, "If You please, Lord." Yahweh then becomes irritated with Moses and tells him, "Is there not your brother, Aaron, the Levite? I know that he is an eloquent speaker. He shall speak to the people for you. He shall be your spokesman and you shall be like God inspiring him." In His mercy, God uses the infidelity of Moses to draw and reserve him for Himself even more, to have him enter into His intimacy even more. God begins to make a friend of him. As Aaron speaks, Moses is to receive inspiration and, in a certain sense, disappear in the eyes of men. We later come to discover how fully this occurs. Moses disappears completely. The mountaintop of Sinai hides Moses as he enters the mystery of God, and when he descends the mountain, his face reflects the glory of God, so much so that the Jews cannot bear the brilliance. God reserved Moses for Himself so much that no one could fix their gaze upon him.

God's education of Moses must be an encouragement for us. The mystery of Mary seems so elevated that it risks frightening us. Moses remains close to us, to what is noble in us. We can

---

128. Mt 1:20

understand his attitude, his fears, the panic that seizes him before God's call. He estimates that what God is asking is too great, that it does not correspond to who he is. How far this is from the simplicity of Mary's heart. What a difference there is between Mary's *fiat* and Moses' bargaining. In Mary, everything is simplicity and humility. She has the heart of a child. She enters fully, without hesitation, into what God expects of her. Moses is somewhat cunning, somewhat wily. He "beats around the bush". He examines the circumstances. He forgets that, before God, there can only be one gaze and attitude: the simplicity of a dove, the very gaze and attitude of Mary at the Annunciation. As with Moses, God educates us so that, little by little, everything in us still of the Old Covenant might yield to the son of God, so that Mary might have us enter the simplicity of her mystery.

We thus grasp all that is divine in the *fiat mihi secundum verbum tuum* [be it unto me according to your word], in the *ecce ancilla domini* [Behold, the handmaid of the Lord]. Moses can be of great help as regards entering more deeply into the mysteries of Mary. The mystery of the Annunciation is the model of the contemplative life in its source. Mary cooperates divinely in how the Father gives His Son. Introduced into the mystery of the Trinity through the gift, she maternally welcomes it. She becomes mother, the mother of the Son of God and, through Him, our mother. Through her, we can understand intimate cooperation with the gift of the Father in faith, hope and love and thus grasp the authentic meaning of Christian contemplation. Mary is the royal path which leads to a fruitful understanding of the gift of God.

Other books available in English
by Fr. Marie-Dominique Philippe, O.P.:

Wherever He Goes: A retreat on the Gospel of John

Available from:

The Congregation of St. John
St. John Priory,
505 Century Drive South
Laredo, Texas 78046-6004
1-956-722-3399

Retracing Reality: A Philosophical Itinerary

Available from:

Continuum Publishers
1-800-561-7704